eat

Nigel Slater is the author of a collection of bestselling books and presenter of five BBC One series. He has been food columnist for the *Observer* for twenty years. His books include the classics *Appetite*, *The Kitchen Diaries I* and *II*, and the critically acclaimed two-volume *Tender*. His award-winning memoir *Toast – the story of a boy's hunger* won six major awards and is now a BBC film starring Helena Bonham Carter and Freddie Highmore. His writing has won the National Book Award, the Glenfiddich Trophy, the André Simon Memorial Prize, the James Beard Award and the British Biography of the Year.

Also by Nigel Slater
The Kitchen Diaries I and *II*
Tender Volumes I and *II*
Eating for England
Toast – the story of a boy's hunger
Appetite
Nigel Slater's Real Food
Real Cooking
The 30-Minute Cook
Real Fast Food

Photographs by Jonathan Lovekin

eat

The little book of fast food

Nigel Slater

Fourth Estate·London

First published in Great Britain by
Fourth Estate
a division of HarperCollins*Publishers*
77–85 Fulham Palace Road
London W6 8JB
www.4thestate.co.uk

A catalogue record for this book is available from
the British Library

ISBN 978-0-00-752615-4

MIX
Paper from
responsible sources
FSC   FSC˘ C007454
www.fsc.org

FSC is a non-profit international organisation established to promote
the responsible management of the world's forests. Products carrying
the FSC label are independently certified to assure consumers that
they come from forests that are managed to meet the social,
economic and ecological needs of present and future generations,
and other controlled sources. Find out more about HarperCollins and
the environment at www.harpercollins.co.uk/green

Typeset by GS Typesetting
Printed and bound in Italy by L.E.G.O. SpA

For James Thompson

Acknowledgements

Early in 1991, I received a letter from Louise Haines, from the publishers Michael Joseph, enquiring whether I had ever considered writing a book. She had read a piece I had written in a magazine and wondered whether we could meet up. I replied that I was flattered and grateful but felt that writing a book was beyond me. Two days later she had talked me into lunch. A meal at which we hatched the idea for my first book, *Real Fast Food*, which was published in autumn 1992. Twenty-one years, ten cookery books, a memoir, a collection of essays and a change of publisher behind us, she remains my editor. I can never thank her enough.

Louise, this book is for you.

To: James Thompson, for his endless inspiration, wisdom, support and friendship. Without you there would be no books, no television series and my life wouldn't be half as much fun. Thank you, sir, for everything.

My gratitude and love also goes to Victoria Barnsley, Jonathan Lovekin, Allan Jenkins, Ruaridh Nicoll, Gareth Grundy, Michelle Kane, Georgia Mason, Olly Rowse, Jane Middleton, Annie Lee,

David Pearson, Gary Simpson, Araminta Whitley, Rosemary Scoular, Sophie Hughes, Richard Stepney at Fourth Floor, Rob Watson and everyone at ph9 and Dalton Wong and George Ashwell at Twenty Two Training. Thank you too to Jenny Zarins for allowing us to use her thoughtful portrait of me. And a big shout out to everyone at the *Observer* and all my followers on Twitter @nigelslater. Thank you one and all.

Introduction

Sometimes we cook purely for the pleasure of it, understanding the provenance of our ingredients, choosing them with great care, thoughtfully taking them on the journey from shop to plate. We seek out the perfect recipe and take our time, lovingly preparing our dinner from scratch. There are times when we might want to take the whole business even more seriously, meeting those who produced it or, if we have the space, growing some of it for ourselves. We want to consider it, discuss it, perhaps even write about it and photograph it.

But sometimes, we just want to eat.

This little book is for those times. The days when we have barely an hour to cook. The times we just want something delicious on a plate at the end of our working day. Yes, we can phone for a pizza, a Chinese or Indian takeaway. We can drop by that Vietnamese place on the way home or pick up a ready-made microwavable delight from the supermarket. But as much as I enjoy the odd takeaway, I have always found dinner is more life-enhancing when I have done more than open a box or picked up the phone. There is much pleasure in making dinner at home, when we have cooked something, however quickly, for ourselves, or for someone else. That is why I have written this book and why its subtitle is *The Little Book of Fast Food*. A collection of recipes that you can have on the table in less than an hour.

By 'fast' I do not mean thoughtless or careless. There is great joy to be had in a perfectly cooked steak, its fat crisping lightly on the grill; a single fillet of spanking fresh fish singing to itself, quietly, in butter; a baked potato whose flesh has been mashed and freckled with rust-red, fat-peppered chorizo. Simple things, done well. Go up a notch and there is a thin, gold and white frittata of goat's cheese; a light chicken ragù with thyme and spring onion; or a broth made with pork ribs and dark stars of anise. Even at its most complex, a Thai vegetable curry is made in minutes once you have blitzed the lemon grass, ginger, chillies, garlic and coriander to a yellow-green paste in the food processor. Making yourself and others something good to eat can be so little trouble and so much pleasure. And much more satisfying than coming home to a meal in a box.

This book
Twenty-one years ago, I wrote my first book, *Real Fast Food* – a collection of ideas and recipes for something to eat that you could get on the table within half an hour or so. Still in print, it is a book of which I am very fond and I wish it well, but looking at those 350 or so recipes twenty years on, I realise how much our everyday eating has changed. How once unusual ingredients are now accessible in every supermarket; how our recipes are more adventurous; the way fresh ingredients are now essential and once frowned-upon shortcuts are now used without apology. *Real Fast Food* is still relevant but our eating has moved on. What seemed new and interesting two decades ago is now everyday. The speeded-up variations of well-known classics still stand, but there are several recipes that now seem somewhat naive, others that are no longer to my taste (we move on) and, if truth be told, there are one or two that should probably never have been there in the first place.

Although I am far from the most prolific of writers, I have

written ten or so books since then, including one or two hefty tomes. For some time now I have wanted to return to the subject of fast food, to update that dear little book and bring it in line with modern eating. That is what you have in your hands. A little book of straightforward, contemporary recipes, quick or particularly easy to get to the table. A collection of recipes that are fast, simple and, I hope, fun.

The recipes
I have every respect for the time-honoured recipe. Those faultless blueprints whose every detail 'must' be adhered to. I appreciate the classic dishes and prefer them to be carried out in their original style rather than tweaked and 're-invented'. That said, I have no wish to eat as if the clocks have stopped, life is too short to attempt perfection every day and to be inhibited by someone else's set of rules. Cooking should, surely, be a light-hearted, spirited affair, alive with invention, experimentation, appetite and a sense of adventure.

The recipes here are straightforward and within the grasp of most of us. I would like to think that many of them will work for those who have never cooked anything in their lives. It is not a book of detailed, pedantic, obsessively honed directions. Written in a short style, they are, I hope, both practical and inspirational. Opposite many of the recipes are ideas that have bounced off them, a scattering of notes, suggestions and narrative recipes that might also interest you. Think of them as little extras.

The recipes are generally for two, but are easy enough to double up. The stumbling blocks of increasing the quantities of ingredients such as gelatine and yeast have no place in this book. Most of the ingredients are fresh but I have taken a few short-cuts, such as using canned beans rather than the dried sort that need soaking and long cooking; the occasional sheet of frozen puff pastry; a tub of decent mayonnaise and even, on a couple of occasions, the ready-made bechamel sauce that you can get in Tetra Paks from Italian delis. These are shortcuts I find useful for everyday cooking.

The form of the recipes is new. Written in the style of an extended tweet, they are no dogged '1-2-3' sets of instructions. The ingredients lists are next to a picture of the finished dish, both at the top of the method so you can see, at a glance, what you will need and then, in more detail, within the method. It is simple enough to get used to.

Some of the ideas in this book are updated recipes from *Real Fast Food*, others from my 'midweek dinners' column in the Sunday *Observer* magazine, and others still started life as tweets to my Twitter followers. Others still have been developed specially for the book by me and James Thompson over the last couple of years. Working in my kitchen at home, we have tested every recipe at least twice and cooked them for photography. They are not all thirty-minute wonders. A few are special-occasion dinners for when you have friends round, and some require minimal preparation but take a full hour or more of unattended cooking in the oven, but the bulk are neat little dinners you can have on the table in half an hour or so and probably even quicker when you have made them once or twice.

We are not chasing perfection here. This is simply a collection of suggestions for something you might like to make for dinner. Just straightforward, delicious cooking. For the times we just want to eat.

Nigel Slater
London, September 2013

www.nigelslater.com
@nigelslater

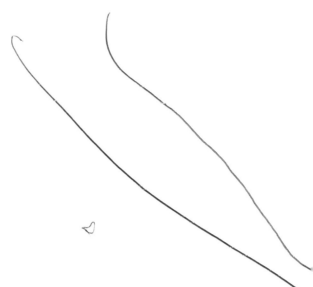

Contents

A quick guide to what to eat by main ingredient

Fish

Meat

Vegetables

Roots

Fruit

Pasta, beans and grains

Eggs and cheese

Leftovers

In the hand

There is an intimacy involved in eating food whilst holding it in your hands. An intimacy you cannot get from the cold steel of a knife and fork or even a pair of wooden chopsticks. The tactile quality of food in the hands is something we get from a sandwich or a wrap (a floury bap; the charcoal dust left on our fingers from a torn piece of warm roti; the cool moistness of a rice wrapper), yet it is a way of life for some cultures, who long ago embraced the art of hand-to-mouth eating.

It is convenient to contain most hand-held food in an edible wrapper – a dough of some sort. It protects our hands from the hot, messy food. A slice cut from a sourdough loaf, a baguette with a shattered crust, a flour-dusted bun, a puckered wrap, an ice-cream cornet, a doughy roti, rye crispbread or thin, skin-like rice wrapper all serve the same purpose. We get to enjoy not only the filling but its wrapper as well. A wrapper that in some cases is warm to the touch and has partially soaked up the moisture from the filling.

The sandwich can be anything from a diminutive, accurately cut cucumber triangle to a doorstop bacon butty the size of an outstretched palm. Matching the bread to the filling can be state-of-the-art or pot-luck, depending on the day. Carefully considered or bunged together, a homemade sandwich rarely fails to hit the spot. Rough pork rillettes on sourdough, goat's cheese on walnut bread, and bacon on white sliced are amongst my desert-island sandwiches, and yes, I do plan for them when I'm shopping. But most are constructed in a somewhat more laissez-faire manner, which is why

I have eaten salt beef on sourdough and Caerphilly cheese on a flat English muffin. (Both good, by the way.)

My rule of thumb is the softer the filling, the more suited it is to a crisp wrapping and vice versa. Which is why silkily wrapped rice paper rolls work so well with their crunchy cucumber and carrot filling and why smoked salmon and soft cream cheese are ideal for chewy bagels. It may also explain the heaven that is ripe Brie with a crackling baguette.

A sandwich needs some form of lubricant. This can be as off the cuff as a trickle of olive oil or as lavish as herb-flecked mayonnaise. It can bring heat (mustard, horseradish or wasabi) or be something more bland altogether, such as fromage frais. Yes, the lubricant – butter, hummus, creamed avocado, goat's cheese, mayonnaise, Patum Peperium, jam, honey, peanut butter – needs to work with the filling but there is plenty of room to experiment. Wasabi and smoked salmon works for me, as does mayonnaise with crisp smoked bacon. Whatever works. We probably shouldn't get too precious about a sandwich, but that needn't mean we can be flippant about it either.

I must mention the burger. From the Big Mac to the now-ubiquitous gourmet burger, the idea of a meat patty held in some sort of bun has long had our attention. The patty is usually pork or beef, but I make them from lamb too, often with cumin and mint, and from sausage meat, mashed beans and shredded vegetables flavoured with mustard seed. The meat can be pure and lightly seasoned or tarted up with an entire spice box. Both have their moments.

In its purest form, a sandwich is something you often make for yourself rather than for someone else. The bread and its filling are ours and ours alone, and we can do as we please. There are no rules. Bread that is less than perfectly fresh can be toasted; fillings can be classic (Cheddar and coarse chutney; roast beef and horseradish) to adventurous (salmon, wasabi and grilled bacon; goat's cheese, peach and black pepper) to downright bizarre. It can be browned in a sandwich toaster or in a film of butter in a shallow pan. Eaten hot, when the melted cheese forms burning strings, or chilled, with ice-cold radishes, cucumber and iceberg lettuce as crisp as broken glass.

The open sandwich has much to commend it. The filling is allowed to tempt the eye more than when it is held captive between two pieces of bread, and it can be more generous too. But a knife and fork are generally involved, taking away that all-important, though far from essential, tactility. An open sandwich – buttery yellow lettuce, smoked trout, dill mayonnaise and cucumber on rye – was one of the first recipes I tweeted. It remains a favourite summer lunch.

I still stand by many of the sandwiches in my first book, *Real Fast Food* (Michael Joseph, 1992): thinly sliced cold roast pork with sea salt, smashed crackling and mayonnaise; bread spread with anchovy paste and Camembert, toasted till the cheese runs; the bacon sarnie made with 'plastic' white sliced bread; even the pitta bread stuffed with fried leftover potatoes, garam masala and basil vinaigrette, despite the leap of faith you need to take to make it.

We all have our favourites. The homemade sandwich is a friend who rarely lets us down. Hand-held food rights our wrongs, turning a bad world briefly good. Here are a few of my favourites, from the simplest to the most extravagant, that continue, year in, year out, to save my soul.

Roast courgette and feta

Slice small courgettes lengthways – longer ones may be better cut into rounds – then put them in a small roasting tin. Toss with olive oil, salt, pepper and a little crushed garlic. Roast till soft and sweet. Crumble over a little feta, then pile into crisp rolls or serve as a warm open sandwich.

Roast vegetables, garlic mayo. The warm, sweet breeze of basil

Slice aubergines, tomatoes and courgettes, toss them in plenty of olive oil, then season with lots of garlic, black pepper, salt and finely chopped rosemary. Roast till everything is very soft. Chop a handful of basil leaves, stir them into mayonnaise and beat in some of the garlicky juices from the roasting tin. Stop before it curdles. Slather the basil mayo over crusty bread, then pile on the vegetables.

The comfort of carbs

Slice leftover new potatoes into thick coins. Fry them in butter and a little oil till they are lightly crisp and golden. Spread mayonnaise thickly on to your bread and pile the hot potatoes on to it. (I like to add chopped dill to this one.)

The Italian
Paper-fine air-dried ham and soft, flour-dusted, airy bread such as ciabatta. I have been known to tuck in a basil leaf or two. You can brush the cut bread with olive oil but the holes prevent the inclusion of any sort of spread.

Steak sandwich

A thin, flash-fried steak. Crisp baguette. Mustard. Mayonnaise. The trick is to slice the bread and press the cut side down into the steak pan, wiping up all the juices with the bread, before adding the mustard, slathering with mayonnaise and tucking the steak in. It's the pan juices that make it.

Buttery leeks and chicken burger

Buy minced chicken, or better still mince your own, so you can include the skin. Slice a spring onion and fry in oil and butter, then add chopped sage, a little garlic and leeks, finely shredded. Let them soften, slowly, under a lid, till they are bright green, satin-soft and buttery. Add the minced chicken and cook briefly, before making into patties and frying in a non-stick pan until golden and sticky. Slather short lengths of crisp baguette with mayonnaise, then use to sandwich the burgers.

Breakfast Burger

sausages, smoked bacon, bagels, tomatoes, cheese

Slit the skin of **3 herby butcher's sausages**, remove the meat and put it into a mixing bowl. Chop **75g smoked streaky bacon**, mix it with the sausage, check the seasoning, then roll into two plump patties.

Using a non-stick pan covered with a lid, cook the burgers in **a little oil**, over a low to moderate heat. Turn each burger several times during cooking, until they have developed a sticky, almost Marmite-like exterior.

Split and toast **a couple of bagels**, place **a couple of slices of large, ripe tomato** and the burgers on the bottom halves, add **a few slices of interesting cheese** and briefly place under a hot grill till the cheese has melted. Top with the other half of the bagels.

For 2. Soft bun. Herby sausage. Smoked bacon. Melting cheese. Happy weekend.

Chicken burger with lemon and tarragon

I can't get enough of these; they're one of my favourite recipes in the book.

Put 400g chicken breasts, with their skin, in a food processor. Add a good handful of tarragon leaves, the zest and juice of a small to medium lemon, a clove of garlic, salt, pepper and 4 heaped tablespoons of dried breadcrumbs (I use panko). Blitz to a coarse paste but stop before the mixture becomes gluey. Heat a fine layer of olive oil in a shallow, non-stick pan, then shape the mixture into about 6 patties and fry for 10 minutes, turning gently, till golden.

The Christmas burger

Fresh white and brown turkey meat, including the skin for succulence, sausage meat (I generally work on a balance of half turkey to half sausage meat), a few chopped fresh or frozen cranberries, fresh thyme, salt and black pepper. Blitz then flatten into small, deep patties and fry slowly in butter and a little oil. Serve with cranberry sauce. Should you decide to use cooked turkey meat for this, mince it well, then add an egg yolk or two to the mixture to help to hold it together.

Duck Burgers

duck breasts, spring onions, plum, honey, soy sauce, breadcrumbs, lettuce, cucumber, chilli

Put **2 duck breasts (about 200g total weight)** into a food processor, add **a large spring onion, a stoned fresh plum, a tablespoon of honey** and **a tablespoon of dark soy sauce**. Blitz to a coarse mince then add **75g fresh white breadcrumbs**.

Form the paste into 4 burgers. Roll each in **a few more breadcrumbs**, then fry over a low heat for 10 minutes each side.

Place each burger on **a large, crisp lettuce leaf**, add **shredded cucumber, chopped spring onion** and **a small, shredded chilli** and wrap the burgers in the lettuce.

For 3–4. Sweet, fruity and crisp.   9

Fish fingers in a sandwich, green herb mayo

Grill or fry fish fingers till crisp. A light cooking should keep them moist inside. Split a baguette in half. Stir some capers, chopped dill and basil into mayonnaise and spread it over the baguette. Tuck in a lettuce leaf, then the hot, fresh-from-the-pan fish fingers. Squirt with lemon juice. Crisp. Soft. Green. Unapologetic.

Trout in a soft bap

Dust a couple of trout fillets in flour to which you have added a good pinch of smoked paprika. Fry in shallow butter, or oil if you prefer, then drain on kitchen paper. Sandwich in a soft, fresh bap and squeeze over a little lemon juice.

Prawns, bacon, brown toast

Grill a few large shelled prawns and some streaky bacon. Put them into a sandwich of hot brown toast spread with a little mango chutney.

Vietnamese Prawn Baguettes

raw prawns, coriander, garlic, chilli, lemongrass,
fish sauce, rice vinegar, pickled ginger, carrot,
ginger, spring onion, mayonnaise, sesame oil,
baguettes

Put **250g raw shelled prawns** in a food processor with **8 coriander stems, 2 cloves of garlic, a bird's eye chilli, a lemongrass stalk, a lump of fresh ginger, 2 teaspoons of Vietnamese fish sauce** and **2 teaspoons of rice vinegar**. Blitz.

Finely shred **half a carrot**. Shred **10g Japanese pickled ginger**. Finely slice **a spring onion** and toss all three together with **a little fresh coriander**. Stir **2 teaspoons of sesame oil** into **2 tablespoons of mayonnaise**.

Put the blitzed prawns in a non-stick frying pan and fry, without any oil, for 4 minutes. Toss with the seasoned carrot. Split **2 small baguettes** and spread with the sesame mayo. Stuff with the prawn hash.

For 2. One of the great sandwiches. IMHO.

Morcilla burger.
Dark blood pudding, white baps

Instead of chorizo, mix 350g soft morcilla with the pork opposite.
Split into 4 and pat into thick burgers. Fry, then stuff into soft, white
baps or sourdough buns.

    Choose a softish chorizo rather than one of the harder varieties. It
should be only a little firmer than a good butcher's sausage.

Pork, juniper.
Breakfast sausage, bright with juniper

Use 650g pork sausage meat taken from good, herby breakfast
sausages. Grind 6 juniper berries and half a teaspoon of fennel seed
in a pestle and mortar, then stir into the sausage meat. You could
include a few herbs, such as oregano, thyme or ground bay. Shape
into 4 thick, flat patties and cook as opposite. Fill the buns with a
fennel salad or a tomato and cucumber salsa.

Chorizo Burgers

chorizo, minced pork, ciabatta buns, salad leaves

Remove the skin from **350g chorizo cooking sausages** and discard.
Put the meat in a mixing bowl, add **250g minced pork** and mix well.
The pork will lighten the dense chorizo. The seasoning will need
little, but much depends on your chorizo, some being more highly
flavoured than others. Split the mixture into 4 and roll into balls. Pat
each one into a thick patty, about the diameter of a digestive biscuit.

Get a non-stick frying pan hot, add **a very thin film of oil**, then
place the burgers in the pan. Let them cook till lightly browned on
the underside, then flip and cook the other side, adjusting the heat
accordingly so they cook through to the middle. Be gentle, lest they
break up.

Split **4 ciabatta (or panini) buns** open, partially fill with **salad leaves**,
then a chorizo burger.

For 4. Smoky, succulent.

Good things to put in your summer rolls,
served with the dipping sauce opposite

- Coarsely shredded daikon, glass noodles, shelled prawns, coriander.
- Shredded red chilli, watercress, beanshoots, sliced roast duck.
- Grilled salmon, cucumber, pak choi, mirin, soy.
- Avocado, tomato, watercress, spring onion, mint.

Summer Herb Rolls

cucumber, red chilli, carrot, spring onion,
rice noodles, spring roll wrappers, mint,
basil, coriander, chives, ponzu sauce, lime,
rice vinegar, hot chilli sauce

Slice **half a cucumber** in half lengthways, scrape out its seeds with a teaspoon then cut the flesh into matchsticks. Very finely slice **a mild, long red chilli**, then cut **a medium-sized carrot** into small matchstick-style pieces. Shred **a spring onion**.

Pour a kettle of boiling water over **50g glass noodles** and let them soak for a few minutes. Moisten **2 large spring roll wrappers** in warm water, lay them on a work surface, then divide the shredded vegetables and noodles between them, tucking **6 or 7 basil leaves, 6 or 7 mint leaves** and **6 or 7 coriander leaves** into each one as you go. Lay **4 slim chives** on to each one, then wrap the vegetables up into parcels.

Make a dip for the summer rolls by mixing together **a tablespoon of ponzu sauce, the juice of half a lime, a teaspoon of rice vinegar** and **a teaspoon of hot chilli sauce**. Eat the rolls, cut into two, with the dip.

Makes 2 large rolls. Bright-tasting. A hot, refreshing crunch.

Cream cheese, smoked salmon

Thickly-cut smoked salmon, generously-spread cream cheese, a golden chewy bagel. Bliss. But try adding a few bottled green peppercorns – the sort that come in brine – to the cream cheese; tuck in a rasher or 2 of very crisp smoked streaky bacon; stir dill or chives into the cream cheese; toast the bagel on its cut sides, spread thinly with wasabi paste then add the cream cheese and salmon; or swap the salmon for mackerel.

Chorizo paste

Peel a soft, salami-type chorizo and blitz it to a paste in a food processor, adding a little crème fraîche or olive oil to give it a spreading consistency. Slather generously on to split and toasted bagels.

The Bagel

bagel, mascarpone, balsamic vinegar,
raisins or sultanas

Put **3 tablespoons of raisins or sultanas** in a small bowl, pour in
2 tablespoons of balsamic vinegar and **2 tablespoons of warm water**
and leave the fruit to swell for 20 minutes or so, then drain, reserving
some of the liquid. Split **a bagel** in half horizontally, lightly toast both
cut edges then brush with some of the soaking liquid from the fruit.

Mix **200g of mascarpone** with the raisins and spread thickly over
the hot bagel.

For 1. Sweet, warm. Feel-good.

Herb Burgers

mung beans, butter or flageolet beans, spring
onions, garlic, basil, chives, parsley, tomatoes,
ciabatta buns, salad leaves, mayonnaise

Drain and rinse **a 400g can of mung beans** and **a 400g can of
flageolet or butter beans**. Finely slice **6 spring onions** and let them
soften in **a tablespoon of oil** over a moderate heat. Don't let them
brown. Peel and crush **2 cloves of garlic** and add them together
with **a large handful of basil leaves, 8 finely chopped chives** and
a handful of parsley, chopped. Tip in the beans and season.

Using a potato masher, partially crush the mixture so there is a
combination of smooth and rough, producing a texture that will be
interesting to eat. Mould small balls of the mixture into thick, flat patties.
You will get about 12. They are fragile so treat them carefully, setting
them down on a baking sheet, then refrigerate for a good 20 minutes.

Warm **a thin layer of oil** in a non-stick frying pan, then place the
patties down in the pan, a few at time, leaving room to flip them over.
When the underside is golden brown, carefully turn the patties over and
cook the other side. Drain briefly on kitchen paper before stuffing them
into **toasted buns** with **slices of tomato, salad** and **a slather of
mayonnaise**. For 6.

Tomato Caesar Bruschetta

tomatoes, Little Gem lettuce, ciabatta,
garlic, egg yolk, vinegar, Dijon mustard

Slice **400g tomatoes** in half and place them, cut-side up, on a grill pan
or baking sheet. Cut **2 Little Gem lettuces** in half and tuck them in
amongst the tomatoes. Season, trickle with **a little oil**, then grill for a
few minutes, till the lettuce has just started to colour and the
tomatoes are soft.

Make the dressing. Peel **2 garlic cloves** and drop them into a
blender. Add **an egg yolk, a tablespoon of white wine vinegar,
a tablespoon of Dijon mustard**, then **4 tablespoons of olive oil**. Blend
till smooth and thick. (You can also do this by hand, in the way you
would make mayonnaise, beating the oil into the other ingredients
with a balloon whisk.) Check the seasoning.

Split **a large ciabatta loaf** and toast it on the cut sides. Place toasted-
side up on a board, trickle over a generous amount of olive oil, then
cover with the tomatoes and lettuce. Spoon over the dressing and eat
immediately, whilst the tomatoes are still hot and the bread is crisp.

For 4. Crisp, sweet, luscious.

Steak sandwich, buttery greens

Heat a well-seasoned or non-stick frying pan over a moderate heat, add a salted and peppered rib-eye steak and let it brown for a couple of minutes, without any oil or fat. Turn and cook the other side, then turn it again a couple of times. Slide a thick slice of butter under the steak – it will melt immediately – and let the meat soak some of it up, then turn it over in the butter, keeping the heat at a temperature that will not let it burn. Remove the steak and let it rest for a good 5 minutes. Melt a little more butter in the pan, add a few thinly shredded spring greens and fry till soft and bright. Split open a baguette, slice the steak into thick strips and stuff into the bread with the hot, buttery greens.

And a messy beef hash

Roughly grate a potato, skin on, then fry it in a little beef dripping with a finely sliced onion until it colours. Add some chopped parsley and thyme. Pour in some of the beef juices from the roast, then add the crisp ends of the roast, bits of golden fat and any interesting crusty bits left behind after the roast has been removed from the tin. When all is sizzling, pile the mixture into bread rolls.

A Beef Sandwich

leftover gravy, cherry tomatoes, roast beef
leftovers, fresh horseradish, mayonnaise,
bread rolls

Warm **the roasting juices and gravy from Sunday's roast beef** over a
moderate heat, including any interesting bits left in the pan. When they
start to bubble, add **a handful of cherry tomatoes**, cut in half, and let
them cook till they colour lightly. Crush the tomatoes in the gravy with
a fork.

Finely grate **a little fresh horseradish** and stir it into some
mayonnaise. Cut **bread rolls** in half lengthways, spread them
generously with the horseradish mayonnaise and fill them with
slices of beef cut from the cold roast. Put dishes of the hot gravy on
the table and dip the rolls in as you eat.

Mozzarella and basil

Split a small ciabatta down its length. Toast the cut sides lightly and spread with basil pesto. Cover with slices of buffalo mozzarella, then stir a little more olive oil into the pesto and trickle it over the cheese. Grill till the cheese melts, but stop before it colours.

Onion, quince paste and blue cheese

Thinly slice a large onion, fry it in a little butter till nutty golden brown, then stir in a tablespoon or two of quince paste. When it bubbles, pile the mixture on to sourdough bread and cover with slices of blue cheese such as Picos, Cabrales or Stichelton.

Labne and mint in pitta

Warm some pitta bread in the oven or under an overhead grill, split it, then stuff with labne, feta (crumbled in a little yoghurt with dried oregano) or goat's curd, plus some mint leaves and a good, thick, sweet olive oil.

Soft cheese, anchovy paste

Spread thin slices of sourdough bread with anchovy paste. Cover with slices of Camembert, Waterloo or similar semi-soft cheese, then add a second slice of anchovy-spread bread on top. Cook on a grill, or place in a frying pan in a little quietly sizzling butter and oil, pressing the sandwich down on both sides till it browns.

Bresaola, Emmental and Pickled Cucumber Sandwich

sourdough bread, bresaola, Emmental cheese, sugar, cucumber, white wine vinegar, Dijon mustard

Lightly peel **half a cucumber** with a vegetable peeler, then halve it down its length and scrape out and discard the seeds. Peel into long, pappardelle-like strips. Put **3 tablespoons of white wine vinegar, 1 tablespoon of Dijon mustard, a teaspoon of sugar** and a little pepper into a mixing bowl and add the cucumber. Leave for 10 minutes.

To make the sandwich, fry **4 very thin slices of sourdough bread** in **butter** till lightly crisp on both sides, then drain on kitchen paper. Pile 2 slices with **thinly sliced Emmental cheese**, shreds of the pickled cucumber, a little salt and **some thin slices of bresaola**. Then add the final slice of bread.

For 2. Toothsome.

With bacon and chilli-coriander mayo

Grill a few rashers of smoked streaky bacon till truly crisp. Finely chop a small chilli, removing the seeds as you go. Fry in a little oil, then stir into 4 or 5 tablespoons of mayonnaise, together with a handful of finely chopped coriander leaves. Pull some cold roast chicken to shreds and fold into the chilli-coriander mayo. Pile the mixture into rolls, tucking the crisp bacon in as you go.

Herb mayonnaise, radish, cucumber

Peel, deseed and dice some cucumber. Trim a few radishes and slice them in half lengthways. Add to the herb mayonnaise opposite with some roughly torn pieces of roast chicken. Pile on to dark rye bread, preferably in a curl of perfect, crisp summer lettuce.

Chicken, Asparagus and Avocado Sandwich

cold roast chicken, basil, tarragon, dill,
mayonnaise, asparagus, avocado, lettuce,
spring onions, sourdough bread

Boil **8 small asparagus spears** in deep water till just tender (they
should still be slightly crisp for this), then drain. Slice them in half
lengthways and set aside. Shred **2 crisp iceberg lettuce leaves**. Trim
4 spring onions and halve lengthways. Peel and slice **a small
avocado**. Slice **a cooked chicken breast**, or remove slices from
yesterday's Sunday roast.

Put **4 heaped tablespoons of mayonnaise** in a bowl, stir in
a tablespoon each of chopped basil, tarragon and **dill** and season
lightly with salt. Toast **4 slices of sourdough bread** and spread each
of them with the herb mayonnaise. Top 2 of the slices with the
lettuce and asparagus spears, followed by the spring onions and
avocado. Place slices of chicken on top and sandwich together with
the remaining bread.

Makes 2 heavily laden sandwiches. Toasted sourdough, herb mayo,
cold chicken, crisp, ice-cold lettuce and avocado. Possibly my
favourite sandwich.

Sweet onions

Fry or grill a seriously good pork sausage. Peel and thinly slice a
couple of onions and let them cook in a little butter till truly soft. Add
a splash of balsamic or sherry vinegar. Add to the sausage as you stuff
it into a roll.

Sausage and cheese

Fry or grill a pork sausage or two. Slice in half and place cut-side up
on a grill pan. Place a slice of cheese – fontina, Comté or some other
firm variety – on top and grill till it melts. Slide into a roll.

Mozzarella Chorizo Sandwich

mozzarella, chorizo, ciabatta, spinach

Slice **130g cooking chorizo** thickly, across the diagonal, then place the slices in a large, heavy based frying pan over a medium heat. There is no need to use any oil or butter. Cook gently for 4–5 minutes, turning halfway through, until the oil begins to escape from the sausage.

Slice **a large ball of mozzarella (about 150g)** on top of the chorizo, then carefully spoon some of the oil from the pan over the top. Cook for 2–3 minutes to allow the cheese to melt – covering with a lid will help – then season with a few twists of freshly ground black pepper.

Tear open **a short ciabatta**, spoon the chorizo and mozzarella inside, then spoon the juices from the pan over the top. Again, there is no need to butter the bread as the pan juices will ensure it gets deliciously moist.

Tuck **a handful of spinach leaves** inside the ciabatta. Give it a good squeeze, allowing all the juices to soak into the bread and the spinach to wilt a little. Slice the ciabatta in half and serve immediately.

For 2. It's all about the juices.

The French

If the bread and ham are of the best quality, then a ham sandwich needs nothing more than a spread of mustard. A perfect baguette, thin, hand-cut ham, a dab of mustard. That is all. If only life was always as simple as this.

The English

There are two sorts of British ham sandwich: the thin, triangular afternoon-tea sandwich, which I am not concerned with here, and the chunkier, more satisfying version. The English farmhouse ham sandwich probably needs thick, impeccably fresh bread, roughly torn ham and a thick layer of mustard. Embellish as you think fit, with lettuce, mayonnaise, tomato or whatever else takes your fancy.

Panini

The delightful little ciabatta-style stuffed bread. Rectangular, shallow, light. The bread is chewy, the filling can be pretty much anything you fancy, but mozzarella often features and crisp, bright green lettuce is pretty much compulsory, as are slices of tomato.

Ham and cheese works. Always has. But try:

- A smear of wasabi on your ham sandwich.
- A brush of green olive paste is worth pursuing.
- Watercress, rocket, basil – peppery things – always cheer up a ham roll.
- A spoonful of creamy scrambled egg makes a substantial twist.
- Warm some thickly sliced bottled artichokes in olive oil and toss them with the ham.
- Brush baby leeks or spring onions with olive oil and grill till soft. Sprinkle with grated Parmesan cheese. Grill once again till the cheese is golden, then pile on top of the ham.
- Fry slices of prosciutto briefly till they curl and crisp, then pile them into soft white bread.

Pork Rillettes, Gherkins and Onion Sourdough

pork rillettes, gherkins, spring onion, sourdough bread

Put **a large spring onion** (2 or 3 if small) in a food processor with **5 tablespoons of olive oil**, add some salt and pepper, then blitz to a green paste. Soak **4 slices of sourdough bread** in this spring-onion oil.

Fry the bread in a non-stick pan till very crisp on both sides. Drain briefly on kitchen paper, then spread 2 slices with **2 tablespoons of pork rillettes** and add **a few gherkin slices**. Top on. Trickle on the last bit of spring onion marinade. Eat.

Makes 2 sandwiches. Sweet-sharp and crisp.

A sort of teriyaki sandwich

Mix together 50ml groundnut oil, 50ml soy sauce, a crushed clove of garlic, 2 tablespoons of mirin, a pinch of sugar and a pinch of dried chilli flakes. Let 2 salmon steaks soak in it for 20 minutes, turning occasionally, then grill till crisp and dark on the outside. Break into large pieces then stuff into split baguettes with slices of cucumber and soft green leaves such as lamb's lettuce.

Chilli-spiced chicken rolls

Cut 400g chicken meat into thin strips. In a food processor whizz a medium-hot, deseeded chilli, a pinch of dried chilli flakes, 2 cloves of garlic, a small handful of mint leaves, the juice of a large lemon and 4 tablespoons of oil to a coarse paste. Toss the meat in the spice mixture and set aside for 20 minutes. Grill the chicken and any clinging marinade till sizzling (there will be quite a bit of smoke) then stuff the hot, spicy chicken into rolls, with watercress or crisp lettuce.

Stir-fried Chicken Baguette

chicken breast, beansprouts, lemongrass, coriander, mint, chillies, ginger, sesame oil, mayonnaise, soy sauce, baguette

In a food processor, blitz the following: **a lemongrass stalk, 2 red bird's eye chillies, a peeled walnut-sized piece of fresh ginger, a handful of coriander, a bunch of mint** and **a little sesame oil.**

Remove the skin from **a chicken breast**, then slice into six. Fry in a wok with **a little oil** till golden. Add the spice paste, let it sizzle then throw in **a handful of beansprouts**. Season **mayonnaise** with **a little soy sauce**. Split **pieces of baguette** lengthways, spread with the mayonnaise, then stuff with the spiced chicken and beansprout mixture.

For 2. Fiery, with the refreshing crunch of beansprout and mint.

Fig and Goat's Cheese Focaccia

figs, goat's cheese, honey, focaccia, rosemary

Split **a piece of focaccia,** about 10cm x 15cm, horizontally to give two rectangles, then place them side by side in a shallow baking tin or oven tray. Set the oven at 200°C/Gas 6.

Pour **4 tablespoons of honey** over the focaccia (if you are using thick honey then warm the jar first in a small pan of boiling water to make it runny). Slice **5 figs** into four from top to bottom and place over the focaccia, then trickle over **another tablespoon of honey** and **a few finely chopped rosemary leaves.** Bake for 15 minutes. Remove and turn the oven to the grill setting.

Slice **10g goat's cheese** into thick rounds and place on top of the figs. Grill for 5 minutes or until the cheese starts to melt. Serve immediately.

For 2. Crisp bread. Melting cheese. Sweet figs.

Jerk burger

Season the burger opposite with a proprietary jerk seasoning – the best of them contain allspice, cloves, cinnamon, thyme and chilli. Fry the burgers, then serve in soft, toasted buns with a little cooked spinach, or if you are near a West Indian market try and get hold of some callaloo.

Gorgonzola, the richest burger

Instead of the ricotta, double up on the beef. Place each burger in your hand and press a ball of Gorgonzola into the centre, then squeeze the meat around it so it covers the cheese. Carefully flatten out into a thick patty then fry as opposite. Soft, toasted buns and slices of ripe tomato complete them.

A burger with attitude

Chop a gherkin. Not finely. Not coarsely. Add it to the mince. Stir in a sprinkling of sesame seeds, a little ketchup, salt and pepper and some hot French mustard. Shape and fry.

Ricotta Burgers

minced beef, ricotta, spring onions, capers,
rosemary, sun-dried tomatoes, sherry vinegar,
ciabatta

Mix together **400g minced beef, 200g ricotta, 4 chopped spring
onions, 1 tablespoon of capers** and **a little picked rosemary**. Season
well with salt and freshly ground black pepper.

Shape the mixture into 6 thick burgers, about the diameter of a
digestive biscuit, then leave for as long as you can in the fridge to
firm up. Fry the burgers in **a little olive oil** in a shallow, non-stick pan
for 6–8 minutes per side.

For the relish, chop **100g sun-dried tomatoes** (the sort that come in
oil) and mix with a little of the oil from the jar. Add **a tablespoon of
sherry vinegar** and season with salt and pepper. When the patties are
cooked, sandwich them between **6 ciabatta rolls** spread with the relish.

For 6. A fresh take on the classic burger.

Tomato Focaccia

tomatoes, focaccia, ricotta, basil, olive oil

Make a basil oil by whizzing **10 basil leaves** and **5 tablespoons of olive oil** in a blender or food processor till you have a bright green dressing. Slice **a couple of large tomatoes** in half and grill till soft and slightly charred at the edges.

Split **a rectangle of focaccia**, about 10cm long, horizontally and brush with some of the basil oil. Grill till lightly crisp. Spread **a large tablespoon of ricotta** on top, then add the tomatoes and trickle over any spare dressing.

For 1. High-summer lunch.

The pork crackling sandwich

Thin slices of roast pork, shredded crackling, a smear of apple sauce.
Roast pork, cut as thick as a pound coin. A russet apple, sliced but not peeled. Gravy. Wholemeal bread, untoasted.

The pork rib sandwich

Slice the meat from last night's barbecue ribs. You will probably get in a sticky mess. Cut the meat into thin shreds then stir into mayonnaise, together with a couple of tablespoons of the barbecue sauce, tasting as you go. Pile a piece of soft, good bread – ciabatta or a bap – with a little shredded carrot or some chopped apple, some tufts of watercress, then pile on top of the pork.

A rare delight (let's face it, it's not that often you have leftover barbecue ribs), but one of the most memorable sandwiches I have ever eaten and one I felt I should share.

Apple pork roll

Finely chop a sweet apple, removing the core as you go. Warm the juices, fat and interesting bits from the roasting tin, then stir in the chopped apple, a dash of cider if needs be, or perhaps a little Marsala. Briefly add thinly sliced cold pork then stuff into a roll, letting the juices soak through the bread. Glorious.

The Sunday Roast Pork Sandwich

leftover roast pork, roast potatoes, crackling and roasting juices, bread, apple sauce

Slice the **leftover pork** very finely and salt it generously. Cut up the leftover **roast potatoes** and warm them in the **juices** from the roasting tin. Spread the **bread** – a panini would be spot on too – with **apple sauce or mayonnaise**. Add the hot roast potatoes, the slices of pork, a bit of **crackling** if you have it and then spoon over the warm roasting juices.

In a bowl

There is much pleasure to be found in a bowl of soup. Cradling our food is a great comfort, especially when it comes in the form of an aromatic liquid such as a steaming broth or thick soup. This is food that instantly soothes and satiates, warms and satisfies. Food that restores.

There is something right about food in a bowl. The hot liquor on your spoon; the warmth of the bowl in your hands; the final scraping of spoon against china – they enable us to feel closer to what we eat. Unlike a plate on a table, we can feel the heat of our food through the porcelain.

The shape of a bowl traps the smell of our food, like a wine glass. As we hold it in our hands and dip in our spoon, fork or chopsticks we experience more of its fragrance: the scent of sweet garlic, warm rice, hot milk, deep broth. Of course we can't cut food in a bowl, and neither should we. The ingredients should be in small enough pieces that no knife is required.

Meals in a bowl are probably at their best when they are simple. I have always loved rice in a bowl. Just plain, white rice. Pure and unsullied. You know you could, if needs be, survive on it. You feel you need nothing more.

But there is more. Oh glory, yes. A little stew of chicken with herbs; a deep, salty broth of beef stock and green vegetables; a spicy laksa; a dahl thick with soft pulses and spice; a Vietnamese-style pho with slithery noodles and coriander. The simplicity of a bowl of golden chicken stock.

Our bowl can be as simple or as elaborate as we wish. A crude earthenware container, a delicate porcelain receptacle, a workaday white soup dish, a piece of ironmonger's enamel, something hand thrown, a family heirloom or something disposable. Whatever we use, it fulfils the same purpose. To hold our food and enable us, should we wish, to cradle it. Comfort food at its most satisfying.

A few favourites

A simple miso broth for a fragile moment
Bring a litre of chicken or vegetable stock or dashi almost to the boil (powdered dashi works well here). Stir in 3 tablespoons of light miso paste, a tablespoon of sesame oil and a couple of tablespoons of soy sauce. Simmer for 3 or 4 minutes, then turn off the heat. To this you can add thinly sliced cabbage or kale, plus paper-fine slices of radish, carrot or fried mushrooms. I like to put coriander in mine, too.

Yellow split peas, spices and tomato
A rich, thick dhal in just over half an hour. Boil 250g yellow split peas in a litre of water for about 35 minutes till almost soft, then drain. In a saucepan, lightly brown a sliced onion in a little oil then add 2 teaspoons of cumin seeds, about 25g ginger, peeled and shredded into fine matchsticks, and 2 cloves of crushed garlic. Stir in a teaspoon of ground turmeric and a pinch of dried chilli flakes, then add a can of chopped tomatoes. Stir in the cooked split peas. Keep cooking for 10–15 minutes, adding vegetable stock or boiling water if necessary, and crushing some of the peas as you stir (or use a vegetable

masher). Finish with a teaspoon of garam masala, salt and some fresh coriander. Eat with warm Indian bread or rice. For 4.

A light, fresh, sweet soup for summer

Separate the leaves of a large soft lettuce. Melt a thick slice of butter in a deep pan, add a large finely chopped shallot and let it soften. Add the lettuce, roughly torn, then stir in 400g peas. Simmer for 10 minutes, then blitz in a blender or food processor in small batches.

The deep savour of beef and noodle broth

Mix together a tablespoon of oyster sauce, a tablespoon of fish sauce, a teaspoon of sesame oil and 2 teaspoons of honey. Brush this over a piece of sirloin steak and grill or cook in a shallow pan, leaving the outside with a dark crust, the inside generously pink. Bring a litre of beef stock to the boil. Pour boiling water over 100g rice noodles and let them hydrate, then drain and place in serving bowls. Slice the steak thickly and place on top of the noodles, scatter with sliced spring onions, chopped coriander, a handful of watercress with its stalks and a little finely chopped red chilli. Ladle over the broth. Season with lime juice. For 2.

Carrot, Black Beans and Coriander

carrots, butter, black beans, coriander leaves, mustard seeds, onion, chilli flakes

Boil **600g carrots** in deep, lightly salted water until tender, then drain, reserving the liquid. Blitz the carrots in a food processor with **20g butter** and 150ml of the reserved cooking water.

Melt **30g butter** in a shallow pan, add **2 teaspoons of mustard seeds** and toast for a minute or two. Drain **two 400g cans of black beans**, add to the pan, cover and leave to cook for 5 minutes, till warmed through.

Peel and finely slice **an onion**. Melt another **30g butter** in a pan, add the sliced onion and fry till golden brown. Scatter in **a large pinch of dried chilli flakes** and a further **teaspoon of mustard seeds**. Sizzle briefly.

Divide the carrot purée between 2 bowls, gently stir in the black beans, scatter over **a few coriander leaves**, then spoon over the sizzling onion and its butter.

For 2. Aromatic, satisfying, sweet and faintly hot.

Split Peas with Aubergine

yellow split peas, aubergine, onion, cardamom
pods, turmeric, cumin seeds, canned tomatoes,
coriander leaves

Soak **100g yellow split peas** for an hour, or longer if you have it. Peel
and roughly chop **an onion,** then let it soften in a deep pan over a
moderate heat in **a little oil.** Crack open **10 green cardamom pods,**
extract their tiny black seeds and lightly grind them in a pestle and
mortar or spice grinder. Stir **a teaspoon of cumin seeds** into the
onion, then add the cardamom seeds. When all is golden and
fragrant, add **2 teaspoons of ground turmeric.** Stir in **a 400g can of
chopped tomatoes** and continue to simmer.

In a separate pan, boil the yellow split peas in deep unsalted water
for about 30 minutes, till soft. Drain and stir into the onion and
tomato mixture. Simmer, stirring regularly, till soft, scarlet and slushy
then season with salt and pepper. Halve and thinly slice **an
aubergine,** then cook in a shallow pan in **several tablespoons of olive
oil** till soft and golden. Drain and stir into the split peas, adding
a handful of coriander leaves. Serve with steamed white rice.

For 2. Rich and earthy. Glowing colours.

Green Vegetable Soup

spring vegetables, white peppercorns, coriander
seeds, turmeric, lemongrass, garlic, ginger,
chilli, coriander, vegetable stock, coconut milk,
fish sauce, lime, soy sauce

Put **a teaspoon of white peppercorns** and **a teaspoon of coriander
seeds** in a dry non stick frying pan and toast lightly for 2 or 3
minutes, then tip into the bowl of a food processor. Add **half a
teaspoon of sea salt, a teaspoon of ground turmeric, 2 lemongrass
stalks**, chopped, **2 cloves of garlic**, peeled, **a 3cm lump of ginger**,
peeled, **3 hot green chillies, 3 tablespoons of groundnut oil** and a
handful of coriander stems and roots. Blitz to a coarse paste. You can
keep this paste for a few days in the fridge, its surface covered with
oil to prevent it drying out.

In a deep pan, fry **3 lightly heaped tablespoons of the curry paste** in
a tablespoon of oil for 30 seconds till fragrant, stirring as you go. Stir
in **200ml vegetable stock** and **250ml coconut milk**, a tablespoon of
fish sauce, and **2 tablespoons of lime juice.**

Add **450g (combined weight) asparagus tips, broad beans** and **peas**
and continue simmering for 5–6 minutes, then shred **a couple of
handfuls of greens** into thick ribbons and add them to the pan.

Finish the soup with **a pinch of sugar, fish sauce, a little soy sauce,
more lime juice** – whatever floats your boat.

For 4. Deep flavours that dazzle. Rich but fresh.

Quiet, old-fashioned flavours for leftover ham hock

Make a crisp, light salad using chicory and inner lettuce leaves tossed with generous handfuls of roughly chopped mint, parsley and basil. Dress with a finely chopped shallot, lemon juice, salt and olive oil. Tear rough chunks of ham from the bone and toss with the dressed leaves. Serve with halved hard-boiled eggs, still quite soft in the middle.

Ham Hock, Herb Sauce

ham hock, peas, garlic, parsley, chives, basil

Put a **500–600g ham hock** in a deep pan with just enough water to cover. Bring to the boil, skim off the froth that rises to the surface, then turn the heat down so the liquid simmers. Cover with a lid and leave, with the occasional turn, for 45–50 minutes or so, till the ham is cooked through to the bone.

Remove the ham from the cooking liquor, add **200g fresh or frozen peas** and **a large clove of garlic**, and cook for 5 minutes or so, till the peas are tender. Add **a handful of parsley**, **a handful of chives** and **a handful of basil leaves** to the peas, cook a minute or so longer, then blitz in a blender to give a thick, green sauce. Add pepper if necessary.

Tear the ham from its bone in large pieces. Roughly chop **a few more of the herbs**, then roll the pieces of ham in them. Spoon the sauce into bowls and add the pieces of ham.

For 2. The nannying quality of peas and ham, the vitality of fresh herbs.

A few thoughts

You could add some cooked noodles if you feel like it, or small pea aubergines that have been halved and lightly fried, or some Thai basil leaves, or other fish instead of the prawns.

Greens and beanshoots. The warmth of coconut and noodles

Put the spice paste opposite into a deep pan, sizzle briefly, then stir in 250ml coconut milk and a litre of chicken stock and bring to the boil. Soak 200g rice noodles in boiling water, drain and divide between 4 bowls. Add a handful of Chinese broccoli or pak choi to the stock. Once it softens, add a handful of beansprouts and a sliced spring onion, then divide between the bowls, ladling it over the noodles. For 4.

Prawns, crisp lettuce and miso. Light, fresh, satisfying

Whisk together 3 tablespoons of white miso paste and 750ml vegetable stock and bring to the boil. Turn the heat down to a simmer and stir in 2 teaspoons each of soy sauce and hot chilli sauce. Shred a couple of crisp white lettuce leaves and their stems and put them in 2 deep soup bowls. Add a finely sliced spring onion and a large handful of cooked prawns to each bowl, then a handful of coriander leaves. Ladle the hot soup over the lettuce and prawns.

Prawns, Lemongrass and Coconut

prawns, lemongrass, coconut milk, coriander,
turmeric, garlic, bird's eye chillies, galangal or
ginger, pak choi, mirin, fish sauce, lime, mint

Put **6 coriander stalks and roots, 2 teaspoons of ground turmeric,
2 large garlic cloves, 2 lemongrass stalks, 2 bird's eye chillies,
2 tablespoons of groundnut oil** and **a thumb-sized knob of peeled
galangal or ginger** in a food processor and reduce to a rough, loose
paste. (This will make twice as much as you need.)

Put half the paste in a pan, fry for a couple of minutes, stirring
regularly, then add **a 400ml can of coconut milk, a head of pak choi,**
cut into large bite-sized pieces, and **8–10 shelled large, raw prawns.**
Bring to the boil and simmer for a few minutes, till the prawns turn
opaque. Finish with **2 teaspoons of mirin, a tablespoon of fish sauce**
and **the juice of a lime**, or to taste. Stir in **the leaves from the
coriander** and top with **a few mint leaves.**

For 2. Vivid flavours, a little heat. Uplifting and energising.

Rib and Rhubarb Broth

small pork ribs, rhubarb, chicken stock, star
anise, peppercorns, bay leaves, spring onions

In a large, deep pan, brown **500g small pork ribs** on both sides in
a little oil. When they are nicely coloured, pour **a litre of chicken
stock** over them, add **2 star anise**, **8 peppercorns** and **a couple of bay
leaves** and bring to the boil. Lower the heat so the liquor continues
cooking at a low simmer and leave for a good 50 minutes to an hour,
keeping an eye on the liquid so it doesn't boil away; you want to end
up with a rich, quite concentrated broth. Check the seasoning.

Remove the ribs from the liquid, pull the meat from the bones and
cut it into chunks (sometimes I leave them whole). Roughly chop
2 spring onions and drop them, together with the meat, into the hot
broth. Pour into bowls. Thinly slice **a small stick of rhubarb** (you may
not need all of it) into long matchsticks and add a few pieces to each
bowl of broth. Serve immediately, just as the rhubarb starts to soften.

For 4. Savoury depth, sharp fruit.

A few thoughts

I often make a chicken broth with the bones from the Sunday roast. The trick is to remember to add all the jelly and bits of savoury goodness that lie under the roasted bird. A 20-minute simmer with a small, halved onion, a few black peppercorns, a tomato and a few parsley stalks will produce a golden-brown broth with deep flavour. The other thing worth considering is the ready-made stocks in the chiller cabinet at the supermarket or butcher's shop. Expensive but often very good indeed.

Chicken wing onion broth

Slice 2 large spring onions and cut lengthways through the bulbs (chop the green shoot). Brown them in a little oil in a wide pan. Add 12 small shallots, peeled but left whole, brown them gently, then remove the spring onions and shallots from the pan. Add 6 seasoned chicken wings and brown on all sides. Add a litre of chicken stock, return the spring onions and shallots to the pan and simmer for 5–10 minutes. Add 100g green noodles and simmer for a few minutes. Season thoughtfully with salt and pepper. Makes 2 deep bowls.

Grilled chicken miso broth

Mix together a teaspoon of fish sauce, a teaspoon of mirin and a tablespoon of hoisin sauce. Brush this over 2 chicken breasts, then cook under an overhead grill till the chicken is cooked through to the centre. Steam or boil 6 stalks of thin-stemmed broccoli, then refresh under cold running water to keep them green. Heat 750ml good chicken stock in a saucepan, then whisk in a tablespoon of white miso paste and a small lump of ginger, peeled and shredded. Slice each chicken breast into 6 and place in 2 large, shallow bowls. Add a little chopped mint and coriander and the cooked broccoli, then ladle the hot miso chicken broth over the top.

Chicken, Asparagus and Noodle Broth

chicken thighs, asparagus, noodles,
mushrooms, garlic, chicken stock

Brown **4 chicken thighs** in **a little oil** in a deep pan. Slice **150g
mushrooms, such as large field, portobello or porcini**, and peel and
slice **2 garlic cloves**. Add the mushrooms and garlic to the pan and
continue browning, adding more oil if necessary. Pour in **a litre of
chicken stock**, bring to the boil and simmer for about 30 minutes. Lift
out the thighs and take the meat off the bones, returning it to the
simmering stock. Shave **4 asparagus spears** into ribbons with a
vegetable peeler, then add them to the soup with **200g noodles**. Cook
for a minute or two, then divide between deep bowls.

For 2–3. Big, generous bowls of noodles. Rich chicken broth. The
sweetness of asparagus.

A sweet and cheering mash

Carrot mash makes a sweet and light accompaniment to any lamb
dish but especially lamb cutlets that have been grilled with rosemary,
steaks fried with thyme and garlic, and any lamb stew where there
are savoury juices to work into the carrot mash with your fork.

Carrot and Bulgur Porridge

carrots, bulgur wheat, vegetable stock, mustard, coriander, butter

Roughly chop **500g winter carrots** and cook them in **a litre of vegetable stock** till tender. Blitz them, together with the stock, in a blender or food processor, then return to the pan over a moderate heat. Add **200g bulgur wheat** and simmer, stirring, for 10–15 minutes, until the wheat is tender. Season with salt, pepper and **a heaped tablespoon of grain mustard**, then finish with **a handful of coriander leaves** and about **40g butter**.

For 4. Somewhere between soup and pilau. Soothing, frugal food for a rainy night.

Another idea from the soup

Butter, short rice, some of the soup opposite, a handful of parsley

Put the soup on to warm. Melt 35g butter in a pan. Add 200g arborio rice, then slowly stir in the hot soup, bit by bit, as if you were adding stock to a risotto, simmering and stirring for 20 minutes or so. Add extra vegetable stock if it appears to be getting too thick, but keep stirring regularly till the rice is al dente.

Remove the flesh from the 2 reserved cooked thighs, and add to the risotto. Stir in 3 heaped tablespoons of freshly chopped parsley.

Artichoke and Chicken Soup

Jerusalem artichokes, chicken, onions, butter

Lightly brown **6 bone-in chicken thighs** in **a little olive or groundnut oil** and remove. Peel and roughly chop **700g Jerusalem artichokes** and **2 onions**. Put them both in the chicken pan with a little oil. Fry for 7–10 minutes till lightly golden, then return the chicken to the pan, add enough water to cover, and bring to a boil and simmer for 30 minutes.

Remove the chicken, reserve 2 thighs for the risotto tomorrow, then slice the meat from the bones of the remaining thighs. Blitz the soup liquid in a food processor or blender. Check the seasoning, then add **25g butter**, stir and pour into bowls. Add the chicken to the bowls.

For 2. Soothing soup for today, risotto for tomorrow.

Roast Chicken Pho

chicken thighs, rice noodles, dark soy sauce,
honey, fish sauce, mirin, ginger, lime juice,
star anise, chicken stock, chilli, greens

Mix **a tablespoon of dark soy sauce** with **a tablespoon of honey, a tablespoon each of fish sauce** and **mirin** and **a chopped red chilli**. Pour into a small roasting tin, add **4 chicken thighs** and turn them over in the mixture till lightly coated. Roast in an oven set at 200°C/Gas 6 for about 25–30 minutes, occasionally turning the thighs over in the honey and mirin. They should be very dark and sticky.

In a saucepan, heat **800ml chicken stock** with **6 'coins' of fresh ginger, 2 tablespoons of lime juice** and **3 star anise**. As it approaches the boil, add **a small handful of shredded greens or chard**, leaving them to cook for a minute or two only.

Put **100g wide rice noodles** in a heatproof bowl and pour over a kettle of freshly boiled water. Leave them to soak for a couple of minutes until they are soft and silky.

Drain the noodles and divide between 2 deep bowls, slice the chicken from its bones and add to the noodles together with the greens, then ladle over the stock.

For 2. Healing broth. Sweet roasted chicken.

A few thoughts

Haddock, gurnard and cod are also suitable candidates for a spiced fish soup.

Rust-coloured, lightly spiced broth, firm white fish

Thickly slice 100g chorizo and cut the slices into thick strips. Cook them in a deep pan over a moderate heat till the oil starts to run and the pieces are sizzling gently. Add a crushed garlic clove and a finely chopped small onion and fry till soft. Stir in a teaspoon or so of chopped rosemary. Tip in 200ml tomato passata and 350ml vegetable stock and bring to the boil. Add 400g hake, haddock or cod, cut into large pieces, and cook for 4 or 5 minutes, till the fish is opaque. Add a handful of chopped parsley, correct the seasoning and serve.

Sour, hot, refreshing. A quick crayfish soup

Sizzle 2 tablespoons of green curry paste in a little oil, then pour in 800ml vegetable stock. Add 4 scrunched lime leaves, or 2 well-bashed stalks of lemongrass, and a couple of coins of sliced fresh ginger. Simmer for 10 minutes, then add 2 diced tomatoes, 300g prepared crayfish tails and a shot of lime juice. As the shellfish warms through, add a handful of torn coriander leaves and a splash of fish sauce.

Spiced Fish Soup

mussels, pollock fillet, mustard seeds,
chilli powder, turmeric, shallots,
cherry tomatoes, coriander

Clean **1kg mussels**, discarding any with cracked or broken shells and any
open ones that refuse to close when tapped on the side of the kitchen
sink. Tug off any wiry beards. Put the mussels in a large, deep pan with
500ml water and bring to the boil. When the shells open, remove the
mussels, reserving the liquid, and take them out of their shells. Discard
any that don't open. Strain the liquid through a fine sieve.

Peel **2 large banana shallots** and separate the layers, then cook
them in **a little oil** in a shallow pan until softened. Add **a tablespoon
of mustard seeds**, **half a teaspoon of chilli powder** and **2 teaspoons
of turmeric** and cook for 3–4 minutes. Halve **12 cherry tomatoes** and
add to the shallots and spices, letting them soften over a moderate
heat for 5 minutes or so. Pour in the reserved mussel stock, bring to
the boil, then lower the heat to a simmer. Cut **250g pollock fillet** into
4 pieces, add to the pan and cook briefly until the fish is opaque. Add
the mussels and **a handful of chopped coriander**.

Enough for 2 generous bowls. Sweet, earthy, spicy.

A leek and clam chowder (an hour of your time but worth it)

Thinly slice 3 leeks, fry in butter till softened, then add 150g smoked bacon, chopped, making sure the leeks do not colour. Cook 1kg small clams with a glass of white vermouth or wine in a large pot with a tight-fitting lid for a few minutes, till the clams open. Pull the clams out of their shells; it doesn't take long when you get into the swing of it. Add 400ml of the clam cooking liquor to the leeks and bacon with 200ml double cream, some black pepper and a little chopped parsley. Remove half of the mixture and blitz in a blender or food processor, then stir it back into the soup. Add the clams and serve with roughly torn crusty bread. For 4.

Sweetcorn and haddock. A cheat's chowder

Fry 2 chopped spring onions in a little butter in a deep pan. Tip in a large can of sweetcorn, 250ml double cream and a handful of chopped parsley. Slide in a couple of pieces of skinned and boned smoked haddock (about 400g total weight). Simmer for about 8 minutes or until the fish will flake easily. For 2.

Spiced Haddock Chowder

haddock, milk, onion, carrot, swede, potato,
mustard seeds, turmeric, bay, parsley, plain
flour, black peppercorns

Cut **2 haddock fillets** in half and place them in a deep pan with **500ml
milk, 2 bay leaves** and **6 black peppercorns**. Bring the milk to the boil
and leave to infuse with the heat off and a lid on.

Roughly chop **an onion** and fry it over a low heat in **a little butter**.
Finely dice **a carrot, a medium-sized swede** and **a waxy, yellow-
fleshed potato** and add to the onion. Fry for 5–10 minutes, till lightly
browned. Stir in **a teaspoon of mustard seeds** and **a teaspoon of
turmeric** and cook for 5 minutes.

Remove the haddock from the milk, reserving the milk. Scatter
2 tablespoons of plain flour over the vegetables and cook for a
couple of minutes. Pour the infused milk into the pan and cook,
stirring continuously, until you have a thick sauce. Place the haddock
briefly in the pan to warm through, then add **a small handful of
chopped parsley** before serving.

For 2. Satisfying. A cold-weather dish.

A few thoughts

- Allowing the miso to boil will make it cloudy and alter its flavour but a brief simmer will do no harm.
- Cook the pieces of meat for seconds rather than minutes, to keep them supple and rare.
- Shredded savoy cabbage, purple-sprouting broccoli and any of the Chinese greens, such as bok choi, would be perfect here instead of the kale.
- Add wide or thin ribbon noodles as you wish, or even cooked rice, to make a more substantial bowl of soup.

Miso Soup with Beef and Kale

white miso, rump steak, cavolo nero or kale, spring onions, bouillon powder

Pull the leaves from the stalks of **100g cavolo nero or kale**. Shred them, then chop the stalks finely. Pour **a little oil** into a shallow pan, add the chopped stems and cook briefly, then add a **240g piece of rump steak**. Fry briefly and when it browns, turn over and add **3 chopped spring onions**. Brown the steak on the other side, then remove from the pan and cover it, then pour **800ml boiling water** into the pan and stir. Add **a tablespoon of bouillon powder** and **2 tablespoons of white (shiro) miso paste**, then the cavolo nero leaves. Simmer until the greens wilt. Ladle into bowls, slice the steak into thin strips and drop into the broth.

For 2. Light and sustaining.

Roasted Beetroot and Tomato Spelt

beetroot, tomatoes, pearled spelt, garlic,
coriander or parsley

Drizzle **4 small beetroot** with **a little oil**, wrap them in foil and place in a roasting tin. Bake at 200°C/Gas 6 for 20 minutes. Open the foil, add **5 garlic cloves**, left whole, and **4 largeish tomatoes** and cook for another 30 minutes, until the beetroot and garlic are tender. Peel the garlic, then peel and halve the beetroot.

Boil **200g pearled spelt** in 400ml salted water for 20 minutes, then drain. Melt **a large knob of butter** in a frying pan, add the cooked spelt and leave to toast lightly for a minute or two. Add the roast beetroot, garlic, tomatoes and some black pepper, stirring them in gently till the tomatoes burst. Stir in **a handful of torn coriander or parsley**.

For 2. Frugal, sweet and sharp, with the comfort of warm spelt.

Pea and Watercress Soup, Prawn Soldiers

peas, watercress, prawns, baguette,
vegetable stock, shallots, soft butter, mace

Peel **2 medium shallots** and chop them quite finely, then let them cook in **a little oil** over a moderate heat, till they are soft and translucent. Tip in **500g (podded weight) fresh peas** then **1 litre vegetable stock**. Stir and leave to simmer for 5 minutes.

Put most of the peas and the liquid into a food processor or blender and blitz till smooth. Add **a bunch of watercress** and continue processing till smooth, then return to the rest of the soup. Making it this way will give you a lightly-textured soup, more interesting than a totally smooth one. Check the seasoning.

For the prawn soldiers, roughly chop **150g shelled prawns**. Cube **50g butter** and mash the chopped prawns into it. Season with black pepper and **a pinch of ground mace**.

Thinly slice **a small baguette**. Spread the prawn butter on to the bread and bake for 10 minutes at 200°C/Gas 6, or cook under an overhead grill if you prefer. Serve with the hot soup.

For 4. Sweet pea soup, crisp prawn toasts.

In the frying pan

You melt a slice of butter in a wide, shallow pan. When bubbles appear around the edge, you slip in a fillet of fish and slowly let it cook, spooning the warm butter over and over. You watch the flesh change from pearl white to snow white and see the edges turn pale gold. You toss a salad or steam some green beans. You open a bottle of wine. You lift the fish on to a warm plate, add a little lemon juice and some chopped parsley to the butter in the pan and let it foam before pouring it over the fish. Dinner is served.

A frying pan was the first piece of kitchen kit I owned. A basic, shallow pan that saw many a meal, from a simple bacon sandwich to a full English. It helped me master everything from fish fingers to fried sea bass. I made risotto and fishcakes in it. Pork chops and hamburgers. Fried chicken and potatoes. I made curry in it, for heaven's sake. If we have only one pan, then it should probably be a frying pan.

Cooking in a shallow, long-handled pan is spirited, high-temperature cooking. A quick fix. We need to learn to control the heat. But first we must know our pan. A thin, cheap pan isn't ideal – the food burns too easily – but sometimes that is what we have. So we should get to know how the pan works, its hot spots and burning points, where food sticks on it and how long it takes to heat up. This isn't just 'chuck it in and hope for the best' cooking. This is quick-fire food, but it needs the right pan, the right heat and the right ingredients.

I have two frying pans now, one cast iron and so heavy I need both hands to lift it, the other non-stick and light as a feather. The cast iron one is so well used it has developed its own non-stick patina, and is what I use to fry potatoes, pieces of chicken, meatballs, burgers and rashers of bacon. It is great for homemade burgers that need slow cooking. The lighter pan is for fish, rösti, frittata and flash-fried lamb's liver. Its slippery surface makes it ideal for an omelette.

If you make them regularly, it might be worth investing in a small omelette pan. Steel is the way to go. Never wash it – just a quick wipe with kitchen paper. A new pan will stick initially. I get round this by heating a film of oil in it and letting it cool several times, then wiping it with paper. This provides a seal that will stop your omelettes and frittata sticking to the surface.

A good, flat pan with a heavy base, whether stainless steel or cast iron, is a food friend to have in the kitchen. For the full English, of course, with its bacon and sausage, black pudding, tomatoes and egg, but for so much more. The pork steak or chop that needs to be watched as it cooks; the steak you don't want to grill; the leftover steamed rice you are resuscitating as fried rice, and for vegetables, chicken and anything else that will cook in a few minutes. It's the lifesaver pan. The one we all start with. The one Mum packs in our backpack when we leave home. Hopefully with a copy of this book.

A few favourites

Sole, asparagus, dill
Melt a thick slice of butter in a non-stick pan and add a little olive oil. Add 6 asparagus spears, each spear cut in half then into 3 or 4 pieces, and let them cook for a minute or two. Scatter in a few roughly torn dill fronds, then lay 2 lemon sole fillets into the pan carefully, skin-side down and side by side, and spoon the asparagus and butter over them. Season, then continue cooking for 4 or 5 minutes, regularly spooning the hot butter and asparagus over the fish until the flesh becomes opaque.

Salmon, spinach, garlic
Fry a piece of salmon in a little oil in a shallow pan, seasoning it with salt as you go. Remove the salmon to a warm place (such as a warm plate with a cover). Put a clove of garlic, peeled and very finely sliced, in the fish pan, let it colour lightly, then add a couple of handfuls of spinach, toss them around in the hot pan, then add a slice of butter and a squeeze of lemon. Serve under the fish.

A sweet, mildly spiced side dish for pretty much anything
Coarsely grate about 400g carrots. Add a crushed clove of garlic, a grated thumb-sized lump of fresh ginger and a finely chopped hot chilli. Melt a little butter in a shallow pan then tip in the carrots, toss gently as they cook, then add a handful of chopped roasted cashews, 4 tablespoons of double cream and the same of yoghurt, then scatter with chopped coriander leaves.

The sweetness of carrots, the coolness of mint

Gently scrub 450g spring carrots, removing their leaves as you go, then cook them in a little oil in a shallow pan. Keep the heat low, rolling them over now and again and letting them brown very slightly in patches. Add 2 tablespoons of chopped mint and 3 heaped tablespoons of yoghurt to the pan. A side dish really, but satisfying enough with bread and cheese or cold cuts.

Potato and mushroom rösti

Grate some potatoes coarsely, then toss them with the beaten egg and flour. Season them with chopped thyme, shape into patties and fry in hot butter till lightly crisp and golden. Drain on kitchen paper for a few minutes, then top with fried sliced mushrooms and crème fraîche.

Rösti and meat juices

Potato rösti are wonderful slipped under grilled lamb steaks or a piece of fillet steak. Something sensational about the crisp tangled straws of potato when they pick up some of the meat juices.

A mustard and tarragon sauce for steak

Put a tablespoon of Dijon mustard, the juice of a lemon and about 20 tarragon leaves in a blender or food processor with 50ml olive oil and blitz to a thick purée. Whilst the cooked steak rests, tip the juices from the pan into the tarragon sauce, blend and serve with the steak.

A red chilli and tomato sauce for steak
While your cooked steak rests, add a deseeded and very finely chopped red chilli to the pan, soften over a moderate heat then add a few chopped tomatoes, some salt and let the tomatoes cook down to a spicy red slush. Crush with a fork, stir in a handful of chopped coriander and serve with the steak.

Rice Cakes

leftover chilled risotto, egg, dried breadcrumbs,
Emmental or Gruyère, lemon

Beat **an egg** lightly in a shallow dish. Tip **a couple of handfuls of
dried breadcrumbs** on to a plate. Cut the **Emmental or Gruyère** into
small dice and fold into your **cold risotto**. Take generously mounded
serving spoons of the mixture and roll into balls or flat patties (the
shape is up to you) then drop them into the beaten egg followed by
the breadcrumbs.

Heat **a shallow layer of oil** in a frying pan and fry the cakes a few at a
time, till they are crisp on all sides, turning carefully (they are fragile)
as you go. Serve 2 croquettes per person with **lemon halves**.

Crunch and soft. Melting cheese.

It is essential to chill the rice quickly for this. Once the risotto is
made, cool it quickly, if necessary by putting the pan into a sink of
cold water. Chill thoroughly in the fridge overnight.

Brussels sprouts, sausage and potato

Cut 200g new potatoes into small coins, about four per potato, then
let them cook in a little oil in a large frying pan. When they start to
colour, add 250g good herby sausage meat in fat lumps, then cut 250g
Brussels sprouts into four and add to the pan. Continue frying till
everything is toasted and the sprouts are soft but bright.

Beetroot with Sausage and Rosemary

beetroot, sausages, carrots, garlic, rosemary,
red wine vinegar

Peel **650g raw beetroot**, cut into thick segments, then cut each segment
in half. Do the same with **150g carrots**, but don't peel them. Peel and
slice **2 cloves of garlic**. Roughly chop the needles from **3 sprigs of
rosemary**. Fry the sliced vegetables, garlic and rosemary in
3 tablespoons of groundnut oil over a moderate heat, till approaching
tenderness (the vegetables need to retain a little crispness).

Cut **400g good, herby butcher's sausages** into three, then add them
to the pan, letting them brown nicely. When the beets and carrots are
tender, pour in **2 tablespoons of sweetish red wine vinegar**, check the
seasoning, adding salt and pepper as you wish.

For 2–3. Sweet and sour, a sausage supper for an autumn night.

A few thoughts

- This is not a recipe where anything should be allowed to brown in the pan. Keep the colours pale and the flavours mild. Rinse the artichokes well of their preserving liquor.
- Tarragon is good here, as it always is with beans, and so would be mint. Add mint at the last minute, so it doesn't discolour much. You could cook your own artichokes if you wish. Prepare and boil them till tender, then add them, halved, to the melted butter and lemon as above.
- Swap the beans for Puy lentils and add more parsley for an earthier style.

Deep-fried artichokes, garlic mayo

Mix 100g plain flour with 2 tablespoons of sunflower oil, 175ml sparkling mineral water and a stiffly beaten egg white to make a tempura batter. Lightly flour then batter halved, bottled or canned marinated artichokes (they're also available loose from delicatessen counters). Lower them into hot, deep oil and fry till light and crisp. Drain on kitchen paper and serve with garlic mayonnaise and half a lemon.

Artichokes and Cannellini

preserved artichokes, cannellini beans,
spring onions, butter, lemon, parsley

Melt **40g butter** in a shallow pan. As it melts, squeeze in the **juice of
half a lemon**. Chop **2 spring onions** and let them soften in the butter
over a moderate heat. Drain **a 300g jar of globe artichokes** then slice
each one in half and add to the butter.

   Drain **a 400g can of cannellini beans** and tip into the pan. Leave to
quietly bubble over a moderate heat till a sort of impromptu creamy
juice has developed. Season with salt, black pepper and perhaps
a little more lemon. Parsley.

   For 2. A 10-minute dish with a gentle quality.

Basil Prawns

prawns, basil, pine kernels, lemon, olive oil

Make the basil dressing: put **20g basil leaves** into a food processor and blitz them to a rich, creamy sauce with **50g pine kernels, the juice of a lemon** and **120ml olive oil.**

Cook **12 large, raw, shell-on prawns** on a griddle or barbecue, or in a dry frying pan. Salt them generously as they cook and turn them regularly till their shells are pink. Remove the prawns from the heat, toss them in the dressing and eat immediately.

For 2. No forks, no knives. Prawns with tasty shells to suck at and flesh to pick.

Classic sausage, cloud-like mash, sweet onion gravy

The classic. Make a quick onion gravy by cooking sliced onions in butter for 15 minutes, until softened, stirring from time to time, then add a little flour, let it colour, and stir in a glass of dry Marsala and enough stock to make a rich, not too thick sauce.

Black pudding, a cloud of potatoes and apples

Boil or steam quite waxy potatoes. Peel, core and slice an equal weight of slightly sharp apples, preferably not as tart as Bramleys, then cook them in a little butter in a shallow pan. When they are soft, fluff them up with a fork. Drain the potatoes and beat them to a fluff with a little butter, then fold in the apple purée. Salt, not sugar. If using soft morcilla, best to bake. A drier, traditional black pudding is better cooked in a shallow pan.

Toulouse sausage, butter bean mash

Grill or fry the sausages. Drain canned butter beans, heat them in a little fresh water, drain, then mash to a soft purée with butter and black pepper.

Chorizo and Sweet Potato Mash

chorizo sausages, sweet potatoes

Pierce **4 chorizo cooking sausages** all over with a fork, then brown in **a little oil** in a shallow pan. Peel about **500g sweet potatoes**, cut them into chunks about the size of ice cubes and add to the pan. Leave the sausages and potatoes to cook for 10 minutes, browning nicely, then add **200ml water**, cover with a lid, and simmer for 10 minutes.

Remove the lid, turn up the heat and allow half the liquid to evaporate, then remove the sausages to a warm place. Mash the sweet potato with a fork, adding **a thick slice of butter** as you go. Season the mash with black pepper and salt, then serve with the sausages placed on top.

For 2. Smoke and silk.

A few thoughts

- Add enough breadcrumbs to produce a mixture that will keep its shape when rolled into balls. You will need slightly different amounts depending on the type of bread you use. Do a trial ball first to make sure they hold together.
- Use a lowish heat, so the crab heats right through to the centre.
- Be gentle when handling the cakes in the frying pan. Leave them to form a crisp crust on the base before carefully turning them over. That way, they should stay intact.

The shimmer of anchovy, the zest of lime

Rinse and finely chop 3 anchovies. Stir them into the crabmeat mixture opposite with the grated zest of a lime.

The warmth of smoke. A fish cake for winter

Use smoked fish such as mackerel instead of crab. Ditch the chilli, and use a beaten egg to hold things together. Dill is better than coriander for this.

Thai style

A little Thai green curry paste, stirred into the crab mixture opposite, produces a dazzling little crab cake.

The ease of canned fish

Sardines and salmon make an instant fish cake but are best when held together with mashed potato rather than breadcrumbs. Use an equal volume of mashed potato and canned fish, then throw in chopped parsley, dill and a little smoked paprika. Drain the fish well before adding it to the potato.

Crab Balls

crabmeat, chilli, garlic, white bread,
coriander, mirin

Put **a hot red chilli**, including the seeds, into a food processor with
a garlic clove, **100g soft white bread** and **a large bunch of coriander**
(about 20g, including both the leaves and the thinner stalks). Blitz till
finely chopped, then tip into a mixing bowl and add **2 tablespoons of
mirin** and **400g mixed brown and white crabmeat**. Season with salt
and black pepper. Mix well, then shape the mixture into 12 small balls.

Warm **a very fine layer of sunflower or groundnut oil** in a non-stick
frying pan, add the crab balls and cook over a low heat till they are
deep golden on the underside. Turn and continue cooking till they
are coloured all over. Serve immediately with **halves of lime**.

For 3–4. Crisp, fragrant dumplings.

A few thoughts

- Keep an eye on the breadcrumbs, they will burn in seconds. Different breads will soak up more or less butter, so keep some extra butter handy to add as necessary.
- As soon as the crumbs turn golden, tip them out into a dish.
- Don't try to fry the courgettes in the pan without wiping it clean and adding fresh oil or butter, as any remaining crumbs will burn.

A change

Introduce some basil in with the courgettes or the crumbs. I went for a passing breeze of garlic but add more if you like.

Mushroom and courgettes, green and earthy

Replace the bacon with small mushrooms that you have sliced thinly, then tossed till dark and sticky in a little olive oil over a moderate heat.

Tomato gremolata

Make the bacon gremolata as opposite. Slice medium-sized tomatoes in half, cook for a few minutes in a little olive oil then scatter the bacon mixture over them. Basil leaves in with the breadcrumb mixture would be a fragrant addition here.

Courgettes with Bacon Gremolata

courgettes, bacon, rosemary, fresh breadcrumbs, parsley, lemon, garlic

Cut **6 rashers of bacon** into thick pieces, then fry them in a shallow pan, with **a little butter** if necessary, till they crisp lightly, then finely chop the needles from **a sprig of rosemary** and add them to the pan along with **a clove of crushed garlic**. Stir for a minute or two then add **a couple of good handfuls of soft, fresh breadcrumbs**. Add **more butter** if the crumbs prove thirsty. Let these cook till golden, turning them regularly, then toss in some **chopped parsley** if you have it, and the **finely grated zest of a small lemon**. Season generously.

When everything is crisp and golden, remove from the pan and wipe the pan with kitchen paper. Slice **4 medium to large courgettes** thickly, then cook them in **a little oil and butter**. When they are soft and translucent, scatter over the crumbs, heat gently and serve. For 2.

Chicken, chickpeas, parsnips. A winter dinner

Not exactly quick, but easy enough. Season 750g chicken pieces and brown them lightly in a little olive oil, then lift them out and set aside. Peel and chop 2 onions and let them soften in the chicken fat left in the pan. Add 6 rashers of smoked streaky bacon, cut into short pieces, and continue cooking till the bacon is pale gold and the onions are soft and sweet. Peel and roughly cube a parsnip, add to the pan with some salt and pepper, then return the chicken to the pan. Add 2 drained cans of chickpeas, pour in a litre of stock and bring to the boil. Cover with a lid, transfer to an oven set at 180°C/Gas 4 and bake for 50 minutes.

Spiced roast chicken, creamy mashed beans

Crush a clove of garlic and put it in a mixing bowl with a teaspoon of dried chilli flakes and 4 tablespoons of olive oil. Toss 4 chicken thighs in the seasoned oil and leave for half an hour. Roast the chicken thighs, seasoned with a little salt, at 200°C/Gas 6 for about 30 minutes.

Meanwhile, drain two 400g cans of cannellini beans, tip them into a saucepan, add 200ml crème fraîche and heat gently. Season with black pepper and salt, then crush with a potato masher to give a rich, creamy mash. Eat with the chilli roast chicken.

Duck with Beans

duck breasts, cannellini beans,
rosemary, dry Marsala

Score the skin of **a couple of duck breasts**, then place them skin-side
down in a hot non-stick pan and fry until golden brown. Drain
a 400g can of cannellini beans and tip them into the pan, turning the
duck over as you go. Tuck **a sprig of rosemary** into the beans and
pour in **5 tablespoons of dry Marsala**. Cover the pan and leave to
simmer for 5 minutes, till the skin is crisp and the flesh is still pink
within. Crush the beans lightly with a fork, season and serve.

For 2. Sweet pink meat, white beans.

A thought

A frittata is cooked a little more slowly than an omelette or scrambled eggs. The filling is usually added as soon as the eggs go into the pan. I give the base a minute or two to set then put the filling on before the centre has time to set.

Asparagus and tarragon

Lightly beat the eggs with a little chopped fresh tarragon. Trim and lightly cook a bunch of asparagus spears – the thinnest you can find, then add to the pan shortly after pouring in the egg.

Aubergine and thyme

Thinly slice a small to medium aubergine into discs. Soak them with olive oil, then scatter with thyme and salt. Cook under a grill or in a griddle, or, if you prefer, fry them in a non-stick pan. They should be really soft and tender. Add to the pan immediately after pouring in the egg.

Goat's Cheese Frittata

goat's cheese, eggs, spinach, butter, thyme,
basil, rosemary

Beat **4 eggs** in a bowl and season generously. Add **a tablespoon of thyme leaves** and **a few roughly torn basil leaves**.

Heat an overhead grill. Melt **50g butter** in a small non stick pan, about 20cm in diameter. Add **150g spinach** and cook for about 1 minute until the leaves soften. Add the spinach to the bowl with the eggs. Wipe the pan, then place **a thin slice of butter** in it. When it starts to sizzle add the egg mixture, then **150g goat's cheese**, sliced, and **a teaspoon of chopped rosemary leaves** and cook on a low to moderate heat.

Once the omelette is partly set – this will take about 6 minutes – finish cooking it under the grill until golden on top.

For 1. A tender, melting omelette.

Ham sandwich, soured cream and mustard mayo

Mix together equal quantities of mayonnaise and soured cream (the cream will sharpen and lighten it a little), then season with smooth Dijon mustard. Add to a classic York ham sandwich with some torn iceberg lettuce and paper-thin, toothsome Cheddar. Crisp, soft and familiar.

Gammon, crème fraîche, two mustards

Fry a couple of gammon steaks in butter, then remove them to warm plates. Add a small tub of crème fraîche to the pan, together with a couple of tablespoons of mustard – I suggest one each of Dijon and grain. Season with black pepper and a very little salt. Bring to a slow bubble, add a squeeze of lemon juice and serve with the gammon steaks.

Gammon Steaks, Broad Beans and Mustard Seeds

gammon steaks, broad beans, butter,
brown mustard seeds

Boil **100g shelled broad beans** in deep, lightly salted water for
8–10 minutes, till tender, then drain them and return to the pan.
Using a fork or potato masher, crush the beans a little.

Melt **75g butter** in a shallow, non-stick pan, let it sizzle, then add **two
125g gammon steaks**. Cook for 3 or 4 minutes on each side, spooning
over the butter as you go. Remove the meat to a warm plate, then add
a teaspoon of brown mustard seeds to the butter and let them cook
briefly – they may start to pop. Stir in the crushed broad beans and a
grinding of black pepper. When all is sizzling, briefly return the
gammon to the pan, then serve with the broad beans.

For 2. Pink meat, green beans.

Some thoughts

- I usually grill marinated meats, but this spiced lamb dish is one you can cook in a pan on the hob. We cooked this with lamb marinated for an hour and also overnight. The difference was negligible.
- Some rice on the side would be good here, perhaps with lemon juice and coriander leaves stirred through at the last moment.
- You could do this recipe with chicken breasts.
- Introduce a little ground cardamom. Finish with fresh coriander leaves or mint.

Harissa

Mix a little harissa paste with enough olive oil to make a thick dressing, then stir in a teaspoon of brown sugar. Spread over the lamb and marinate for half an hour or longer if you have time.

Red wine vinegar, garlic, crushed rosemary

Crush a clove of garlic, mix it with a little salt, some finely chopped rosemary, black pepper and a touch of red wine vinegar. Rub this over the lamb, then grill.

Lamb with Yoghurt and Turmeric

lamb steaks, garlic, fennel seeds, turmeric, ground coriander, yoghurt

Set aside **4 lamb steaks, about 200g each**. Peel and crush **a large clove of garlic** and pound it with a pestle and mortar with **half a teaspoon of fennel seeds**, then add **a teaspoon of turmeric** and **a teaspoon of ground coriander** and a little black pepper. Put **250ml yoghurt** into a mixing bowl, then add the spice paste and mix well. Put the lamb steaks into the yoghurt and leave for an hour or so.

Remove the steaks from the yoghurt and fry in **groundnut oil** in a hot, shallow pan, still with some of the spiced yoghurt sticking to them, till a crust has developed, then turn and cook the other side. Serve with rice.

For 4. Earthy. Aromatic. Fragrant.

A few thoughts

- At the time of writing, monkfish isn't particularly sustainable, but any other firm white fish is suitable. Keep the pieces large and cook them only briefly.
- If the pan seems a little dry, add a trickle of olive oil before adding the fish.
- Once the clams go in, put the lid on the pan to encourage them to steam quickly. They are cooked as soon as they open. Discard any that don't open.

Brick-red chorizo, sweet mussels, a little vermouth

For a change, fry some chopped chorizo in a deep pan, add the fish, as in the recipe opposite, and replace the clams with mussels in their shells, plus a little vermouth or dry sherry and just a little coriander leaf. Cook, covered, until the mussels open.

Adding a rouille

Make a quick, cheaty rouille by stirring paprika and a little garlic purée into a good brand of mayonnaise. Add it to the dish as you serve it.

Monkfish with Pancetta and Clams

monkfish, pancetta, clams, smoked paprika, white vermouth

Cut **100g smoked pancetta** into large dice, then cook in a shallow pan over a moderate heat. As the fat starts to run and the pancetta colours a little, toss **four 200g pieces of monkfish tail** in **2 teaspoons of smoked paprika** mixed with a little salt and pepper. Add the pieces of fish to the pan and cook for 7–8 minutes, turning them as necessary. They need a little colour on each side. Wash **200g small clams**. Pour **250ml white vermouth** into the pan, let it bubble up, then add the clams. Cover the pan with a lid and cook briefly until the shells start to open. Discard any that remain shut. Check the seasoning and serve.

For 4. Pan juices that dazzle.

The richness of liver, the sweet-sourness of apple chutney

Warm a thin slice of butter and a glug of oil in a shallow pan. Lay
4 slices of lamb's liver in the sizzling pan, fry for a couple of minutes
on each side (toasty brown edges are good, but the inside should still
be rose pink). Remove to a warm plate and pour a small glass of dry
Marsala or red wine into the pan. Bubble, stir and scrape then reduce
by half over a high heat. Stir in 4 tablespoons of coarse apple and
onion chutney. Slide in the liver and serve.

Lamb's Liver, Onions and Pecorino

lamb's liver, banana shallots, radishes,
red wine vinegar, parsley, butter, Pecorino

Peel, halve and very finely slice **300g banana shallots**. Melt **40g butter**
in a large, non-stick frying pan. Add the shallots and fry, stirring
regularly for about 10 minutes till soft and pale golden. Push to one
side of the pan.

Cut **300g lamb's liver** into small pieces and season generously.
Add **a thin slice of butter** to the pan, then add the liver and fry for a
maximum of 2 minutes on each side. Add **5 thinly sliced radishes**.
Pour in **2 tablespoons of red wine vinegar** and add **a handful of
parsley leaves**. Then add **50g finely grated Pecorino**. Serve with
skin-on mashed potato.

For 2. Good for you.

Aubergine Paneer

aubergine, paneer cheese, cherry tomatoes,
garam masala, yellow mustard seeds,
coriander

Warm **2 tablespoons of sunflower or groundnut oil** in a shallow pan
or wok. Cut **a large aubergine** into small dice (about 1cm), add to the
oil and fry until golden and soft. As the aubergine colours, halve
200g cherry tomatoes and add them to the pan. As they soften, tear or
chop **250g paneer cheese** and add that to the pan too. Scatter over
a tablespoon of garam masala, a tablespoon of yellow mustard seeds
and a little salt. Continue frying for a couple of minutes, till the paneer
is very lightly coloured, then stir in **a handful of coriander leaves**.
Serve with steamed rice.

For 4. Cheerful, singing flavours.

Parsnip Rösti

parsnips, potato, banana shallots, balsamic
vinegar, egg, goat's curd or cream cheese,
plain flour, sugar, green peppercorns

Peel **8 banana shallots**, slice them in half and unfurl the layers. Warm
a thin slice of butter and **4 tablespoons of olive oil** in a shallow pan,
add the shallots and fry over a low to moderate heat till soft and pale
gold. Stir in **3 tablespoons of balsamic vinegar** and **a tablespoon of
sugar.** Cook over a low heat until the shallots are sweet and sticky,
then set aside but keep warm.

Coarsely grate **250g parsnips** and **a medium potato** into a bowl.
Lightly beat **an egg** and add it to the bowl with **2 tablespoons of plain
flour.** Mix well and press the grated vegetables into 6 small, thin
patties. Heat **a thin film of groundnut oil or butter** in a frying pan,
add the patties and fry till crisp and golden. Remove, drain briefly on
kitchen paper and divide between plates.

Season **250g goat's curd or cream cheese** with **a few bottled green
peppercorns**, a little black pepper and some salt. Place a heaped
spoonful of the curd on top of each pancake and add some of the
warm shallots. Serve immediately. For 3–4.

A few thoughts

This is a dish born from an empty store cupboard and to add too
many ingredients would miss the point. A chopped chilli at the start
would add interest, as would a handful of torn basil at the end. Other
appropriate additions include chopped or sliced garlic, added with
the onion, a pinch of ground paprika, some fennel seeds or a little
smoked garlic. An egg or two, cracked on top at the end, will bring all
the ingredients together.

Poor Man's Potatoes

potatoes, peppers, onion, vegetable stock

Wipe **500g new potatoes** and halve them. Heat **a little olive oil** in a shallow pan, place the potatoes in it cut-side down and leave them to cook. Halve and deseed **2 large yellow or red peppers**, cut them into long strips and add to the pan. Peel and finely slice **a large yellow or red onion** and add it to the potatoes and peppers, together with **a large knob of butter**. Leave to cook, with the occasional stir, until the potatoes are nicely golden and the onion is starting to soften. Pour in **400ml vegetable stock**, bring to the boil, season, then cover with a lid and let it simmer enthusiastically for 20 minutes. Once the stock has almost disappeared, crush a few of the potatoes with a fork, allowing them to absorb the last drops of liquid.

For 2. Frugal, rich, nourishing.

Lamb and leeks

Sweat a couple of finely sliced, medium-sized leeks in butter till they are soft but not coloured. This is often done with a layer of greaseproof paper over the leeks and a lid, so they sweat as much as fry. Grill or fry a lamb steak, slice into thinnish strips, then toss with the cooked leeks and a little grated Caerphilly cheese. Serve over boiled fettucine or tagliatelle.

Grilled duck and red onions

Peel and slice a couple of red onions, then let them cook in a little butter and oil till soft. Grill or shallow-fry a duck breast till tender, slice into thin strips, then toss with the onions, a tablespoon of red wine vinegar and a handful of chopped parsley. Serve with the pasta.

Philly Cheese Steak with Tagliatelle

skirt steak, tagliatelle, provolone picante cheese, onions, beef dripping

Peel and thinly slice **2 medium onions** and fry them to a soft, pale gold in **2 tablespoons of oil** or **preferably beef dripping**. Cook **150g tagliatelle** in a deep pan of salted water, then drain. Grate **180g provolone picante**. Slice **250g skirt steak** into finger-thin strips, then add to the onions, letting the strips cook briefly, keeping their insides pink. Toss the steak, onions and pasta then add the grated provolone picante and a little black pepper.

For 2–3. Intensely satisfying. Piquant and good value.

A few thoughts

- Make certain the chops brown nicely on both sides before you introduce the cider; that way the pan juices will be tastier.
- Use figs that are lightly ripe so they don't collapse during cooking. If you have tiny ripe figs you could leave them whole.
- Include a little chopped thyme or rosemary with the chops.
- Swirl a knob of butter into the juices at the end.

The sweetness of pork chops, the glow of translucent pears

Cook pork chops in a little butter and oil in a shallow pan. As the chops start to colour, add sliced, unpeeled pears and continue cooking till tender and translucent. Remove the chops and fat, then add a small wine glass of both vegetable stock and perry or cider, reduce by bubbling, then spoon over the chops. On the side? A salad of chicory and walnuts.

Ripe plums, rosemary

Finely chop a tablespoon of rosemary leaves, then mash them with a thick slice of butter, a little salt and some black pepper. Melt half of the butter in a shallow pan, then, once it starts to sizzle, add 2 large pork chops and let them colour nicely on both sides. Keep the heat moderate to low whilst they cook right through. As the chops approach the end of their cooking time, add 4 halved and stoned plums and the rest of the rosemary butter. Once they are soft and the pork cooked, serve.

Pig and Fig

pork chops, cider, figs

Season **2 pork chops**. Melt **a little butter** in a shallow pan and once it starts to sizzle, brown the chops on each side. The fat should colour nicely. Pour in **250ml dry cider**, let it bubble, then lower the heat, halve **4 small figs**, add them to the pan and cover with a lid. Continue cooking for about 5 minutes, then remove the lid and let the cider reduce by about half.

For 2. Sweet, succulent, fruity.

Pistachio, pumpkin, pumpkin seed

Fry pumpkin instead of potato, steaming it for a few minutes first, then add pumpkin seeds and shelled pistachios for a bit of crunch.

Roast artichoke, walnut and egg

Jerusalem artichokes can be peeled, steamed, diced and browned in butter, then scattered with chopped walnuts and salt. Slide a fried egg on to the plate.

Potatoes with Hazelnuts and Egg

new potatoes, hazelnuts, egg yolks, butter, chives

Wash and roughly chop **500g new potatoes**. Warm **75g butter** with **a couple of glugs of groundnut or olive oil** in a shallow pan over a moderate heat, add the potatoes and fry at a gentle sizzle till golden brown all over and tender. Roughly chop **100g hazelnuts**, add them to the potatoes and let them colour a little. Season lightly with salt and black pepper. Add **4 tablespoons of chopped chives** and tip into a heatproof dish.

Separate **4 eggs**, dropping the yolks into the potatoes, then place under a hot grill for 3 or 4 minutes, till the yolks are warm but not set.

For 2. The scrunch of hazelnuts.

A few thoughts

- Choose the smallest pork ribs you can find – sometimes known as baby back ribs. They need to cook quickly.
- Watch carefully when browning the ribs, and when adding the marinade to the pan, as they can burn easily. Keep the heat moderate.
- Try the same marinade for larger ribs and bake them slowly in a low oven. Serve with rice or bread for mopping up any sauce.
- This recipe works with chicken drumsticks too. Just cook them for a little longer.

A red fruit version

Use cranberry jelly in place of the pomegranate molasses. Add a little crushed juniper and a splash of cranberry juice and cook as opposite.

Aniseed and honey

A traditional rib recipe might include black treacle, cayenne pepper, mustard powder, tomato ketchup, onion, garlic, smoked paprika, cider vinegar and apple juice. The only way to find the perfect ratio for you is to keep tasting as you go along. My knee-jerk rib recipe is mostly honey, to which I add half the amount of oyster sauce, then plenty of crushed garlic, some dried chilli flakes, a little ground star anise, salt and black pepper. It works best as a long, slow bake, but also in the version opposite.

Quick Pork Ribs with Honey and Pomegranate Molasses

baby back pork ribs, honey, pomegranate molasses, dark soy sauce, dried chilli, mirin

Mix together **3 tablespoons of honey, 2 tablespoons of dark soy sauce, a teaspoon of dried chilli flakes, a tablespoon of pomegranate molasses** and **2 tablespoons of mirin**. Slice **300g small pork ribs into individual ribs**, then toss them in the dressing.

Brown the ribs quickly in **a little oil** in a shallow pan over a moderate heat, turning them regularly. As soon as they start to caramelise, pour over any remaining marinade and let it bubble briefly, taking care not to let it burn, then add **100ml water**. Cover the pan with a lid and cook for about 5 minutes. Remove the lid and continue cooking for a couple of minutes, till the ribs are dark and glossy.

For 2. Sticky, spicy, fingerlicking stuff.

Black pudding frittata

Melt a thick slice of butter in a small non-stick frying pan. Remove the skin from 200g black pudding and crumble the pudding into the hot butter, leaving it to colour to a deep golden brown. Lightly beat 3 eggs, add about 3 tablespoons of roughly chopped parsley, then pour the mixture over the black pudding. Add 50g finely grated Parmesan cheese. Cook over a fairly low heat till the bottom has formed a golden crust. The centre will hopefully still be wobbly. Slip the pan under a hot grill till the frittata has set and the top is lightly coloured. Cut into wedges to serve.

Spiced Root Frittata

parsnip, beetroot, carrot, onion, cardamom, cumin, coriander, dried chilli flakes, black mustard seeds, canned tomatoes, eggs, plain flour

Peel and grate **250g (total weight) of mixed root vegetables, such as parsnip, beetroot and carrot**. Peel, then finely shred **a small onion** and add to the grated roots. Stir in **2 tablespoons of plain flour, half a teaspoon each of ground cardamom, cumin and coriander, a pinch of dried chilli flakes** and **half a teaspoon of black mustard seeds**. Mix in **half a can of chopped tomatoes**, drained. Lightly beat **4 eggs** and add those too.

Warm **a thin pool of butter** in a 20cm shallow non-stick pan, then add the egg and tomato mixture. Cook till a golden crust has formed on the base but the top is still quite liquid in the centre, then place under a preheated overhead grill and cook for 2 minutes or so, till lightly set.

For 2. A soft tangle of sweet vegetables held together by lightly spiced eggs.

Salmon with Artichokes

salmon, preserved artichokes, parsley,
dill, lemon

Grill, bake or shallow-fry **350g salmon**, then set aside. Slice
4 preserved grilled artichokes in half.

Flake the cooked salmon then warm in **a little olive oil** in a shallow,
non-stick pan. Add the artichokes then season with **whole parsley
leaves, a little chopped dill** and **a squeeze of lemon**.

For 2. Light, clean, delicate.

Sweet potatoes, the crunch of nuts

The recipe opposite works very nicely with sweet potatoes cut into small cubes. Once the potatoes are soft inside and are starting to colour, toss in a few cashew nuts, let them colour lightly, then add chopped chives and the crumbled sardines.

Earthy artichokes, a spritz of lemon

Slice well-scrubbed Jerusalem artichokes in half and fry them in butter and a little oil till they are soft inside and crisply golden on the outside. Add a generous amount of chopped parsley, a can of drained and broken-up sardines and a good squeeze of lemon juice.

Sardines, Potatoes and Pine Kernels

canned sardines, new potatoes, pine kernels,
spring onions, parsley

Scrub **400g new potatoes** and quarter them. Brown the potatoes in
a heavy-based frying pan in **a little olive oil**. This will take a good
15 minutes at a low to moderate heat with the occasional stir.

Chop **3 spring onions** into rings and roughly crush **30g pine
kernels**. When the cut sides of the potatoes are crusted and golden,
add the spring onions and cook briefly till soft. Add **a large handful
of torn parsley**, the pine kernels and a little black pepper. Lastly, drain
100g canned sardines in olive oil, letting them crumble a little, and
add to the pan.

For 2, as a light meal. Crunchy nuts, toasted potatoes.

A few thoughts

- Get a good sausage. Perhaps something with plenty of parsley and pepper in it. To peel them, slit the skin from one end to the other with a knife, pull the skin apart and squeeze the filling out into a bowl.
- Beef up the seasoning a bit if you like, with some chopped thyme, crushed garlic, black pepper or grated Parmesan.
- Use a good-quality ready-made stock. Supermarkets and some butchers have it in sachets or tubs.
- Add chopped dill to the meatballs and the sauce.
- Use crème fraîche instead of cream or, for a less rich dish, use just stock and forget the cream.
- For a milder version use chicken stock instead of beef.
- Serve with wide ribbon noodles such as pappardelle.
- Instead of using shop-bought sausages, season plain sausage meat as you wish. Try juniper, thyme, garlic, cumin or ground cardamom.

The freshness of lemon, the warmth of rosemary

Season the mixture opposite with very finely chopped rosemary, crushed garlic and a little grated lemon. Shape into balls, fry in olive oil, adding a little butter and lemon juice to the pan juices at the end.

Sausage Balls, Mustard Cream Sauce

sausages, beef stock, double cream,
Dijon mustard, chives

Remove the skins from **450g really good-quality butcher's sausages**.
Roll the sausage meat into about 24 balls, slightly smaller than a golf
ball. Warm **a little oil** in a non-stick frying pan over a moderate heat
and cook the balls till they colour, turn them over and continue
cooking till they are evenly browned. Tip away any excess fat and
pour in **500ml beef stock**. Bring to the boil, allow to reduce a little
then pour in **250ml double cream** and stir in **a tablespoon of Dijon
mustard**. Season with salt and pepper and continue cooking for
15–20 minutes. Remove the balls to warm dishes, turn the heat up
under the sauce, there will be lots of it, and let it reduce a little. It
will not thicken. Pour the sauce over the meatballs and serve with a
fork and a spoon for the sauce. **A few snipped chives** can be added if
you wish.

For 2–3. My favourite meatballs, ever.

Spelt with pork

Brown a pork chop, either from the loin or neck, in a little oil. Add a diced apple – it's quite good with the skin left on – and a couple of leaves of sage. Tip in the pearled spelt, then pour over vegetable or chicken stock and simmer for about 25 minutes, till the spelt has swelled and the chop is tender.

Spelt risotto

Use pearled spelt in place of rice in a risotto. Melt a thick slice of butter in a pan, add a finely chopped shallot, some pearled spelt, then stir in hot stock as if you are making risotto. Work on 200g of pearled spelt to 1 litre of hot stock. Mushrooms would be good here, chopped into plump nuggets and fried with the shallot, before you add the spelt. Finish with grated goat's cheese.

Spelt, Basil and Ricotta Cakes

pearled spelt, ricotta, egg yolks, basil, tomatoes

Boil **250g pearled spelt** in deep, lightly salted water for 20 minutes, drain and set aside.

Stir in **250g ricotta, a couple of egg yolks, 20g whole basil leaves**, salt and black pepper. Leave for 15 minutes then shape into eight round patties. Fry gently in **a little olive oil** in a non-stick frying pan until golden and crisp on the outside. If they appear to be browning too quickly then lower the heat a little and cover with a lid. Serve with **thick slices of ripe tomato** and **a trickle of olive oil**.

Makes 8 small patties, enough for 2–4. Gentle and mild, but with big peppery bites of basil.

A classic

Roll the mince mixture opposite into balls. Seal them in a little oil in a shallow pan over a moderate heat, then transfer to an ovenproof dish. Pour tomato sauce over them, then bake till the sauce is bubbling and the balls are cooked right through.

Mushrooms, cream. An autumnal version

Make half the quantity of lamb mixture opposite and mix it with the same amount of ricotta cheese. Shape into patties and fry in a little oil, then remove from the pan. Fry sliced chestnut mushrooms in the pan until golden, adding more oil if you need to, then pour in a little brandy and scrape up the stickings from the base of the pan. Add crème fraîche or double cream. Stir, simmer for a minute or two, then pour the mixture over the patties and bake for a few minutes to cook the meat right through.

Mint and sultanas. The crunch of pine kernels

Add fresh or even dried mint to the minced lamb mixture opposite, plus a few golden sultanas and some pine kernels. Shape into patties and fry all the way through, then remove from the pan. Add a good thick slice of butter and some lemon juice to the pan, stir to scrape up the tasty pan-stickings, then tip the mixture over the patties and serve.

Spiced Sesame Lamb with Cucumber and Yoghurt

minced lamb, black mustard seeds,
white sesame seeds, spring onions,
garam masala, cucumber, yoghurt, mint

Put **500g minced lamb** in a bowl, add **a tablespoon of black mustard seeds, 4 tablespoons of white sesame seeds**, salt, pepper, **2 spring onions**, chopped, and **2 teaspoons of garam masala**. Mix well, then divide into 8 and flatten into large patties, about the thickness of a digestive biscuit.

Heat **a little olive oil** in a shallow, non-stick pan, place the patties in it, cooking approximately 2 at a time, and fry for a minute or two on each side, till patchily golden.

Take long, thin shavings from **a cucumber** with a vegetable peeler and season with a little salt and pepper. Stir **a tablespoon of chopped mint** into **4 tablespoons of yoghurt**.

For each person, place a patty on a warm plate, top with a few curls of cucumber and a spoonful of yoghurt, then add another patty.

For 4. Savoury, aromatic lamb cakes, a trickle of yoghurt.

A few thoughts

- Steaming or boiling the squash before frying ensures it is truly tender and fluffy.
- Keep the heat moderate when cooking the spices, so they do not burn.
- Keep the eggs lightly cooked; the runny yolk forms a dressing for the squash.
- Serve with sausages instead of eggs. Try with parsnips or main-crop carrots instead of squash. Use the spiced squash as a side dish for grilled chicken, or stir it into a pilau.

Buttered poached eggs and herbs

Melt 50g butter in a shallow pan. As it bubbles, slide in 4 lightly poached eggs. Scatter them with a couple of tablespoons of chopped herbs and a few drops of lemon juice and baste gently. Serve immediately.

English muffins, cheese, poached eggs

Toast and generously butter split English muffins. Top them with poached eggs, pile on grated cheese, then bake or grill till melted.

Eggs and ham

Same as above but place a piece of York ham under the poached eggs and use sliced provolone cheese on top of them.

Spiced Eggs with Squash

squash, mustard seeds, garam masala, eggs

Peel **a medium-sized squash, such as onion squash or butternut**, and remove and discard the seeds. Cut the flesh into small bite-sized pieces. Steam the squash over boiling water till tender to the point of a knife, then drain and set aside.

Warm **4 tablespoons of olive, rapeseed or groundnut oil** in a deep frying pan, then add **a tablespoon of mustard seeds**. Add the cooked squash and let it colour. Stir gently, taking care not to break up the pieces, then sprinkle over **a tablespoon of garam masala**. Continue to cook for a few minutes, till fragrant, then remove to 2 warm plates. Break **2 eggs** into the pan and fry till just cooked. Slide them carefully on top of the squash.

For 2. Sweet, autumnal.

Steak with Miso

rib-eye or rump steak, white miso paste, shallot,
tarragon, chervil, cider vinegar, butter

Fry **2 rib-eye or rump steaks** in **a little butter and olive oil** in a shallow
pan, turning and basting regularly (I turn mine every 2 minutes and
baste almost continuously). When the meat is done to your liking, lift
from the pan and set aside to rest on a warm plate. Add **60g butter** to
the pan, let it sizzle briefly, then stir in **a shallot**, finely chopped, and
let it soften for a minute, stirring occasionally and scraping the
browned steak juices from the pan. Add **2 tablespoons of white (shiro)
miso** and **a tablespoon of cider vinegar** and whisk. (If it looks like the
sauce is splitting, add **a spoonful of hot water** and whisk.) Stir in
a tablespoon of chopped tarragon and **a tablespoon of chopped chervil.**
  For 2. Steak with deeply savoury juices.

James's Potato Tortilla

egg, potato, shallot

Cut **an unpeeled medium to large potato** into very, very small dice
– a *brunoise*, as they say in cheffy circles. Melt **a thick slice of butter**
in a small, shallow 15cm pan. Add the potatoes and cook till soft and
pale gold, about 10 minutes. Add **a banana shallot**, peeled and very,
very finely sliced, and cook for 3–5 minutes to soften. Beat **an egg** with
seasoning, then pour it over the onion and potato. Cook for about
3 minutes, until it puffs up round the edges, then finish cooking it
under a hot grill, leaving it liquid in the centre.

For 1. A potato, a shallot, a little butter and an egg.

Of all the recipes James and I have worked on together, this is the
one that I think of as his and his alone. There is something quite
perfect about it. Maybe it's the Spanish in him. Whatever, this is one
of the loveliest things I have ever eaten.

Tomatoes, Charred Onions
and Steak

rump steak, butter, spring or salad onions,
tomatoes

Melt **60g butter** in a very large shallow pan and season a **450g piece
of rump steak** with salt and black pepper. When the butter is sizzling,
brown the meat on both sides, remove and set aside. Cut **3 large
spring or salad onions** in half lengthways and add them to the pan,
letting them brown a little.

Halve **650g large tomatoes**, then add them to the pan, covering
with a lid and letting them cook for 10–15 minutes or so till soft and
lightly browned here and there. Season generously, pressing the
tomatoes lightly with a spoon so their juices run into the pan.

Now that the steak has rested, slice the meat thickly, then tuck the
pieces amongst the softening tomatoes. Continue cooking briefly,
then serve.

For 2–3. Raw meat, ripe tomatoes, pan juices.

A few thoughts

- The mango should be ripe, but not so much so that it is too tender to cook. Otherwise it will fall off the skewers.
- If mango doesn't tempt try plums, they go very well with pork.
- I have used pork shoulder with great success, but any cut will work, although the fatty cuts will produce a lot of smoke if cooked under the grill.

Lip-tingling pork, cool pomegranate-flecked yoghurt

Coarsely grate half a small cucumber then put into a colander and season generously with salt. Leave for 20 minutes, then squeeze out the excess water. Fold the cucumber into 200ml yoghurt, then stir in a small handful of fresh mint leaves, the seeds from half a pomegranate and a generous grinding of black pepper. Thread 200g cubed pork steaks on to flat wooden skewers. Using a pestle and mortar, mash half a teaspoon of sea salt flakes, a quarter teaspoon of black peppercorns and a large, peeled clove of garlic to a coarse-grained, wet powder, then rub all over the pork. Trickle lightly with olive oil, then grill, browning nicely on all sides. Eat with the pomegranate yoghurt.

Miso pork kebabs

Put a lightly heaped tablespoon of light (shiro) miso in a small saucepan over a moderate heat. Pour in 3 tablespoons of mirin, then stir until the miso has dissolved. Toss the cubes of pork in the mixture, then thread on to wooden skewers and grill till the edges are deep glossy brown, turning from time to time.

Greengage and honey

Brush the cubed pork with a mixture of honey and Dijon mustard and season generously with salt. Thread on to wooden skewers, alternating pork pieces with greengages. And cook as opposite.

Pork and Mango Kebabs

pork shoulder, grain mustard, mango, lemon

Cut **400g pork shoulder** into large cubes, about 3cm in diameter. Put them in a dish with **a tablespoon of oil** and **2 tablespoons of grain mustard**, add a grinding of black pepper and plenty of salt and mix thoroughly so that each piece of meat is covered with a light coating of mustard.

Peel **a ripe mango**. Remove the flesh from the stone in the largest pieces possible, then cut into large cubes, roughly the same size as the meat. Thread the pieces of meat and mango on to wooden or metal skewers, pushing the pieces close together.

Brush **a thin film of oil** over a heavy, non-stick or cast-iron frying pan and place over a moderate heat. When the oil is hot, place the skewers in the pan and let the meat colour appetisingly, then turn and cook the other side. Check that the meat is cooked right through, then serve. (You may find a palette knife useful to slide under the meat and mango where it sticks slightly to the pan.) A fat squeeze of **lemon** will make it sing.

For 2. The warmth of mustard. The lusciousness of mango.

On the side

Rice, plainly steamed. No spice.

Chicken, light soy, smoky chilli flakes, the warmth of maple syrup

Mix 2 tablespoons of maple syrup with 1 tablespoon of light soy sauce and another of lemon juice. Stir in 2 large pinches of crumbled dried chilli flakes. Baste the grilling chicken pieces with this as they cook.

Crunchy wings, garlic mayo, fingers to lick

Dust the wings with seasoned flour and deep- or shallow-fry till the outside is crisp. Drain briefly on kitchen paper, then serve with a pot of garlic mayonnaise.

Citrus and heat, one for chilli heads

Whizz a whole clementine, with its skin, in a food processor with as much habanero chilli as you can take (they are very, very hot), a little mild mustard, then red wine vinegar and sugar to taste. If you add too much chilli, chuck in another clementine. Pour into a saucepan, bring to the boil, then simmer till thick. Blitz, boil down, and use as a marinade for chicken wings before grilling or roasting.

Chicken Wings, Katsu Sauce

chicken wings, onion, ginger, garlic, carrots,
tomatoes, honey, soy sauce, garam masala,
curry powder, chilli, chicken stock

In a food processor combine **a peeled onion, a cork-sized piece of
peeled fresh ginger, 3 cloves of garlic, 250g carrots, 350g tomatoes,
3 tablespoons runny honey** and **3 tablespoons of soy sauce**. Mix in
2 tablespoons of garam masala and **2 tablespoons of mild curry
powder** and **a small, hot red chilli**. Blitz to a paste, then fry for
5 minutes. Add **12 chicken wings** and brown lightly, adding **a little
groundnut or sunflower oil** if necessary, then pour in **400ml chicken
stock** and simmer for 30 minutes.

Remove the wings to a non-stick frying pan and cook over a
moderate heat to crisp them. Serve with the sauce.

For 2. Crisp little wings. Hot sweet gravy.

Smoked salmon, soured cream, dark rye

Mix together equal quantities of soured cream and mayonnaise, then season with salt, pepper and a few capers. Peel a sweet red onion and slice it into very fine rings. Spread the soured cream mixture on to squares of sticky dark rye bread, add a little of the onion (taking care not to add too much), then cover generously with smoked salmon. Top with a second piece of rye bread or serve open.

Smoked trout, wasabi

Mash some smoked trout into a coarse paste with a fork. Add about half the amount of cream cheese, then mix in a good squeeze of wasabi paste, a shot of lemon juice and a little salt. Keep tasting and adding more wasabi until it is hot enough for you. Spread thickly on sliced farmhouse bread and cover with a single layer of very finely sliced white daikon or radish. Then spread over the smoked trout paste. I like to use a light, moist brown bread for this one.

Smoked mussels, gherkins

Finely slice a couple of large shallots and cook in butter in a shallow pan. When they are soft, sweet and pale gold, add a couple of coarsely sliced large gherkins, then a tin of smoked mussels, drained of their oil. Sandwich in 2 small, floury baps.

Potted Shrimps, Cucumber, Dill and Sourdough

potted shrimps, cucumber, dill, lemon, sourdough bread

Tip **150g potted shrimps** into a non-stick frying pan and let them cook briefly in their butter. Peel **half a cucumber**, slice it very thinly with a vegetable peeler, then toss with **a handful of torn or chopped dill**. Add **a good squeeze of lemon**.

Grill **2 large slices of sourdough bread**, then top with the shrimps and cucumber. For 2.

Herb Ricotta Cakes

ricotta, eggs, flour, butter, chives, chervil,
parsley, avocado, lemon, sprouted seeds

Make a topping for the cakes. Halve, peel, stone and finely dice **an avocado**, put it in a bowl, then add **the juice of a lemon**, a little black pepper and **a couple of glugs of olive oil**. Cover and set aside.

To make the ricotta cakes, separate **3 eggs**, putting the whites into a bowl large enough to beat them in later and the yolks into another bowl. Add **250g ricotta** to the egg yolks, then stir in **50g plain flour** and **30g melted butter**. Chop **a handful of chives**, **chervil** and **parsley** and stir them in, then season with a little salt.

Beat the egg whites till light and fluffy, then stir into the ricotta mixture. Melt **a little butter** in a non-stick frying pan over a moderate heat. Take a sixth of the ricotta mixture and pat it lightly into a small cake, about the circumference of a digestive biscuit, using the back of a spoon. Make 2 more. When the butter sizzles lightly add the cakes. When the cakes have coloured lightly on the base, flip them over with a palette knife (do this quickly and confidently and they won't break), then let the other side become a soft, pale gold. The full cooking time shouldn't be more than a few minutes. Repeat with the remaining mixture.

continued

Remove the cakes with a palette knife or spatula, rest briefly on kitchen paper then transfer to a plate. Place **a heaped tablespoon of ricotta** on each cake, divide the avocado mixture between them, then add **a few sprouted seeds** and serve.

Makes 6. Light, tender, fresh little pancakes.

A few thoughts

Once the rice is soft and tender, add the lightly beaten egg. The trick is to leave it in place for a minute or so for the egg to partially set, before stirring and breaking it up amongst the rice. It is easy to overcook, so once the egg has had its initial setting time, stir briefly and regularly to break it up and distribute it evenly amongst the rice.

Green spiced rice

Use green curry paste instead of the red. Before you add the carrot and rice to the pan, fry a few sliced button mushrooms in the butter, letting them colour lightly. At the very end, fold in a little chopped cooked spinach, or perhaps some cooked peas. Broad beans will work if there are no edamame.

Fridge rice

Although I don't believe fried rice should ever be used along with any old leftover you might find lurking in the fridge, it is nevertheless a good way to use up leftover sausages, thinly sliced bacon and finely chopped cooked greens. The trick is never to add more than one type of leftover at a time.

Quick Spiced Rice

basmati rice, Thai red curry paste, edamame
beans, carrot, vegetable stock, eggs, coriander

Cook **150g podded edamame beans** in boiling water, then drain
and set aside. Pour **400ml vegetable stock** into a saucepan, add
2 tablespoons of Thai red curry paste, then **200g white basmati rice**.
Bring to the boil, cover with a lid and leave to simmer for 10 minutes
till almost tender and most of the liquid has been absorbed.

Melt **a slice of butter** in a frying pan, add the rice together with **a
large carrot**, coarsely grated, and the reserved edamame beans. Stir
regularly till the rice is moist but no longer wet, then add **3 eggs**,
lightly beaten. Season. Continue cooking, leaving the rice in place for
a few minutes to let the egg colour, then stir it gently to break the
mixture up. Carry on for a couple of minutes till the egg is lightly
cooked and visible in patches throughout the rice. Toss in **a handful
of coriander**.

For 2–3. A little lifesaver.

Root Vegetable Patties
with Spiced Tomato Sauce

parsnips, carrots, onion, egg, cardamom, cumin,
coriander, dried chilli flakes, black mustard
seeds, canned tomatoes, garlic

Mix together **a scant teaspoon of ground cardamom, half a teaspoon
of ground cumin** and **half a teaspoon of ground coriander**. Stir in
a large pinch of dried chilli flakes, a teaspoon of black mustard seeds
and **a tablespoon or so of groundnut oil**. Toast half this spice mix in
a pan for a couple of minutes. Crush **a garlic clove** and add to the pan
with **a 400g can of chopped tomatoes** and a little salt. Simmer for
10 minutes.

Peel and grate **250g parsnips** and **250g carrots**. Peel **a small onion**
and shred it finely. Mix the onion with the grated roots and
2 tablespoons of plain flour, then lightly beat **an egg** and stir it in.
Mix in the remaining half of the spice mix and squish the mixture
into 6–8 shallow patties. Fry them in a shallow, non-stick pan in
a little oil over a moderate heat till lightly crisp, then turn and
continue cooking briefly. Serve with the spiced tomato sauce.

For 2, as a hearty meal. Crisp, spicy.

On the grill

I have a rectangular, ridged iron griddle. It sits on top of the gas jets of the hob and is where I often cook my steaks, lamb cutlets and boned chicken pieces. I brown slices of aubergine on there too, and spring onions and young, skinny leeks. It produces clouds of smoke, which need an efficient kitchen extractor if they are not to set off the smoke alarm. The food that comes from it is the most delicious of all: a little singed, sizzling and glistening with oil and caramelised sugars. It is one of the most used pieces of kit in my kitchen.

I try not to wash my griddle very much, preferring to wipe it with kitchen paper. A wet griddle or griddle pan will rust. A new one will stick. But as it gets older, the patina (posh word for burnt-on grease) protects the iron and the washing becomes less of a problem. Even then, it should be dried quickly and put away if it isn't to get rust patches. I also use the overhead grill in my oven. This produces a different effect, as the food doesn't directly touch the heat, but it has been the source of many a daily dinner.

Ideally, I would grill my food over charcoal. But that must be done outside and I'm not about to go into battle with charcoal and matches after a day's work. It has to be said that a griddle or overhead grill will never quite produce the same flavour as when food is cooked over charcoal. Nevertheless, food grilled indoors can be pretty damned good. I like the direct heat of the griddle – the charring, the smoke, the slightly primitive flavours that ensue.

This grill chapter is short and sweet: some cutlets, a couple of ideas for chicken and a pork chop. Yet these are the recipes I probably use most during the week. Grilled meat, a bowl of salad, a glass of wine. Dinner, as good as it gets.

A few favourites

Sweet roast garlic, soft butter, French bread

Wrap a head of garlic in foil with a little oil and thyme and bake for 40 minutes or so. Squeeze the cloves out into a bowl and roughly mash with a little butter and salt. Grill a couple of boned chicken legs, and when almost done, spread the surface of the meat with the roast garlic butter. Serve with a baguette, torn into rough, crackle-crusted chunks, on the side for mopping up the butter.

Scallops, fresh chilli

Mix scallops with olive oil, finely chopped mild red chilli and a little coarse black pepper and leave to marinate for about half an hour. Thread them on to wooden skewers, alternating with large chunks of peeled and deseeded cucumber. Grill and serve with rocket leaves, fresh coriander and lemon.

Berbere lamb. The mystery of long pepper, nigella, chilli and basil

Rub lamb cutlets with olive oil and dust with a commercial Berbere spice blend. Grill, then serve with a salad of orange and mint.

Grilled prawns, garlic mayo
Peel, then crush a clove of garlic with a little salt, beat in 2 egg yolks and a squeeze of lemon juice, then slowly, drop by drop at first, whisk in 125ml groundnut or sunflower oil and 125ml olive oil. Toss whole, raw, shell-on prawns in a little groundnut or sunflower oil then grill till pink and sizzling. Serve with garlic mayonnaise.

The ancient scent of za'atar and olives
Season lamb steaks or cutlets with olive oil, salt and pepper. Halfway though grilling, dust with za'atar – the dry mix of thyme, savory, sumac and sometimes sesame, sold in Middle Eastern grocer's shops – and add a little more olive oil. Continue grilling for a few minutes, taking care that the spice does not burn (its usual use is to season flatbreads). Scatter with green olives and finish with a squeeze of lemon.

Black garlic and olives. A breath of southwest France
Squeeze a head of the black garlic out of its skins and mix to a thick paste with a little olive oil. Stir in some finely chopped black olives and thyme leaves, then spread it over lamb cutlets or steaks and grill.

I find the most satisfying way to grill chicken is to take a boned leg and cook it on a hot, ridged griddle. Boning a chicken leg is easy. A thigh even more so. Place the meat, plump-side down, on a chopping board. Make two deep cuts with a small, sharp knife following the two bones. Weedle the knife in and out, slicing the flesh away from the bones, until you have two clean bones and a rough rectangle of chicken flesh. Keep the skin on.

Chicken with thyme and sea salt, butter, lemon

Melt butter and add chopped fresh thyme leaves. Grill the boned and flattened chicken leg as in the recipe opposite. As the chicken grills, brush it with the butter. Once the chicken is golden on both sides and the skin a little crisp, scatter with sea salt flakes and finish with a generous squeeze of lemon.

Dark soy and golden honey, chilli fire

Stir a very finely chopped hot red chilli into an equal mixture of dark soy sauce and honey and brush this over the chicken as it grills. Offer halved limes at the table.

Miso chicken – possibly my favourite fast-food recipe ever

There, I've said it. In a small saucepan, warm together 6 tablespoons of mirin, 2 tablespoons of shiro miso and a little oil. Toss the boned chicken thighs in the mixture, making sure they are well coated, then cook under an overhead grill, basting regularly till the skin is golden and crisp.

Citrus Chilli Grilled Chicken

chicken legs, lime, lemon, chilli flakes

Remove the bones from **2 chicken legs** with a small sharp knife, then place each rectangle of meat on a piece of cling film, fold the film over the meat and bat out with a rolling pin so it increases by half of its original size.

Make several narrow slits through the skin and the meat with the point of a sharp knife, going about halfway through the meat. Rub a scant teaspoon of sea salt flakes into the skin and down into the cuts. Grate the **zest of a lime** and the **zest of a lemon**, rub them into the skin, then do the same with **a large pinch of dried, crumbled chilli flakes**.

Place the chicken, skin-side up, under a high grill, adding **a little oil** only if it looks a little dry, and cook for 6–9 minutes, till sizzling and golden.

Squeeze **the juice of the lime** and **the juice of the lemon** over, season generously with sea salt and eat immediately. Soft bread and butter. A rice pilaf maybe.

For 2. Feisty chicken.

Grilled Lamb
with Minted Feta

lamb cutlets, feta, mint, yoghurt, garlic

Put **6 tablespoons of olive oil** in a shallow dish, then peel and crush
a clove of garlic and stir it into the olive oil with a grinding of salt
and pepper. Put **6 lamb cutlets** into the olive oil and turn them over
to cover them with the oil. Leave in a cool place for an hour or longer.

To make the minted feta, put **200g feta cheese** into a food
processor and blitz briefly. Add **4 tablespoons of yoghurt**, **10 or so
mint leaves** and a few twists of black pepper, then blitz again for a
few seconds, till you have a thick cream. Scoop into a bowl with a
rubber spatula and refrigerate till needed.

Cook the cutlets under or over a hot grill till the outside is golden
brown, the bones a little charred and the inside rose pink. Remove
the cutlets from the grill and place on warm plates with large
spoonfuls of the feta cream.

For 2. Forks not required.

A few thoughts

- Umeboshi plums are expensive and not something you will find at the corner shop, but I love this little recipe. Wholefood shops and Japanese food stores are good places to look for them. Make no mistake, these plums are unrelentingly salty and sour and you will not want to add any salt to the chutney. Start with a small amount of sugar and increase it to your taste, but don't lose the salty-sourness.
- Cook the onions down slowly so that they are really sweet and soft before you add the umeboshi. The longer and slower the better.
- This would make a good glaze for pork ribs too.

Chicken Wings with Onion Umeboshi Chutney

chicken wings, onion, umeboshi plums, sugar

Peel and slice **a large onion**, then let it soften in **a tablespoon of groundnut or rapeseed oil** in a shallow pan over a moderate heat. While it is cooking, remove and discard the stones from **200g umeboshi plums** and chop the flesh.

When the onions have started to turn a honey colour, add the umeboshi and **100ml water**. Continue cooking for 10 minutes then sweeten a little with **sugar**, to taste. Start with a teaspoon and continue till the sauce is salty, sour and sweet. Simmer down till thick and gloopy. Turn off the heat and set aside.

In **a little oil**, fry **12 large, free-range chicken wings** till golden all over, then add them to the plum and onion mixture and stir them so that they are lightly coated.

Get an overhead grill or barbecue hot. Place the wings, a little sauce adhering to them, on a grill pan and cook till lightly crisp and golden brown. Serve with the remaining umeboshi and onion mixture to dip.

For 2–3. Salty, fruity, curiously addictive.

A thought

Long pepper is a softly aromatic peppercorn available from spice dealers.

Sweet and garlicky

Stew thinly sliced red peppers, fresh or from a can, in olive oil with thinly sliced red onion and garlic. The longer you cook, the sweeter and stickier it becomes. Finish with basil and serve with the chops.

Pear, walnut, shallot, vermouth

Peel a large banana shallot, halve lengthways and unfurl, then cook in butter in a shallow pan. Cut a pear into thick slices and as the shallots soften, add to the pan, then add a few thinner slices of pear so they break down into a slush as they cook. Toss in a few walnuts. Lastly, pour in a splash of white vermouth. Cook for 5 minutes more, then serve with the chops.

A savoury side

Fry a chopped shallot in olive oil, add a little chopped anchovy and let it break down, then add thinly sliced button mushrooms and chopped parsley.

Pork Chop with Plum Chutney

pork chops, plums, onion, juniper berries, cloves, sugar, long pepper, red wine vinegar

Peel, halve and slice **a large onion** into thick segments. Remove and discard the stones from **500g plums**. Put the onions and plums in a deep pan and add **4 crushed juniper berries, 2 cloves, 3 tablespoons of caster sugar, 2 tails of long pepper** and a generous grinding of salt. Simmer over a low to moderate heat for about 15 minutes, then add **3 tablespoons of red wine vinegar** and check the seasoning. Grill **4 pork chops** and serve with the warm chutney.

For 4. Sweet meat, pickled plum.

A few thoughts

- Small lamb cutlets do not need to marinate for long – 15 minutes or so will do.
- Choose quite lean cutlets to avoid too much smoke when grilling.
- Let the bones brown and even char a little; they are good to pick up and eat.
- Use thick coconut cream in tins. If you want to use the thick variety in packets, then moisten it with a little boiling water first.

A pork version

Pork, cut into thick finger-like strips, can be substituted for the lamb. Add about a teaspoon of cumin seeds to the spices. Include a little chopped spring onion or fine shallot. Use thick yoghurt instead of the coconut cream. Serve with roughly chopped coriander leaves.

Lamb Cutlets with Mustard Seed and Coconut

lamb cutlets, coconut cream, ground coriander, black mustard seeds, garlic, ginger, cabbage

Spoon **160ml coconut cream** into a shallow bowl. Add **2 teaspoons of ground coriander**, **2 tablespoons of black mustard seeds** and a grinding of black pepper. Peel **2 cloves of garlic** and chop finely. Peel **a thumb-sized piece of fresh ginger** and shred it, matchstick style, then stir both the garlic and ginger into the coconut cream. Roll **6 lamb cutlets** in the coconut cream and leave for 15 minutes.

Heat a griddle pan or overhead grill and cook the cutlets till lightly golden brown. Expect quite a bit of smoke. Shred **300g Savoy or other dark-leaved cabbage** then fry quickly in **a little butter or oil**.

For 2. Sizzling chops.

A thought

Golden beetroot seem less sweet to me than the more common red
varieties, but it could just be my imagination. Either is suitable for
mashing. The heat of the fresh horseradish is pleasing with the sweet
earthiness of the beet.

Pan-fried haddock, parsley sauce, olive oil and lemon mash

A parsley sauce for shallow-fried haddock, made by simply adding
crème fraîche to the pan once the fish is cooked, along with a handful
of finely chopped spanking fresh parsley and simmering for a minute
or two. Serve with a loose mash made from waxy potatoes, olive oil
and lemon juice (add the lemon juice to the olive oil before mixing
with the potatoes).

Smoked haddock, bacon, cabbage mash

Grill or bake the smoked haddock. Cook the bacon, then make a
mash with coarsely chopped cabbage and potatoes.

Salmon, creamed green peas

Boil and drain green peas, then blitz them to a purée with butter and
a few leaves of mint. Serve with baked or grilled salmon.

Grilled Kippers, Beetroot and Horseradish Mash

kippers, beetroot, fresh horseradish, butter

Scrub, but do not peel **4 medium-sized red or golden beetroots**, then boil them whole in deep, lightly salted water for 30 minutes or so, depending on their size. They must be truly tender. Skin them – you should be able to slide the skin off with your thumb – then trim them neatly before returning them to the pan and crushing with a potato masher. Beat in **50g butter** with a wooden spoon, seasoning with salt and **2 tablespoons of grated fresh horseradish**.

While the beets are cooking, get a grill or griddle pan hot, then lightly brush **2 kippers or 4 fillets** with **oil** and cook for about 3 or 4 minutes on each side. Alternatively, cook them in a shallow pan with **a little butter**. Serve alongside the beetroot and horseradish mash.

For 2. Smoky fish, sweet beets, hot radish.

Couscous, Lemons, Almonds, Squid

couscous, lemon, preserved lemon, salted
almonds, squid, green olives, lime, parsley

Plump up **125g couscous** in twice its volume of freshly boiled water or
stock into which you have squeezed the juice of **a lemon**. Add the
empty lemon halves to the couscous for flavour. Chop **a preserved
lemon** into tiny dice, discarding its pulp. Mix with **a handful of
toasted salted Marcona almonds, a handful of stoned green olives,
a little lime juice** and **lots of chopped flat-leaf parsley** and add to the
couscous. Finish with black pepper and just a shake of **very fruity
olive oil.**

Score **500g prepared squid** lightly with a sharp knife, then cut into
large pieces. Grill for a couple of minutes, till lightly cooked, the
surface a little charred here and there. Place on the couscous.

For 2. Warm grains of couscous. Grilled seafood. A spritz of fresh
lemon.

On the hob

My first flat had no oven, only a couple of electric rings on which to cook dinner. Pretty good some of them were too: little vegetable curries, lamb stews, sautéed chicken and endless, endless pasta suppers. Dishes cooked on the hob, in a high-sided frying pan or deeper saucepan, are generally things that take longer than the frying-pan dinners of the earlier chapter. The deeper pans allow you to cook in liquid and in larger quantities. You can boil fettuccine or simmer meat in a sauce; steam basmati or stir a soup.

For the most part, these are dishes cooked in a single pot that will sit over gas or electric heat at a rolling boil, a calm simmer or quietly plodding towards tenderness. Most, though not all, require a lid of some sort. We are talking fried chicken with bread sauce, slow sautés with their pan juices, a stirred risotto, clams cooked in their own steam. And then there's pasta of course: tangles of pappardelle and little pasta shapes that hold a sauce; there is couscous, lentils and beans.

We cover food with a lid to keep its liquid from evaporating, to allow it to cook a little more slowly than in a shallow open pan, giving it time to cook right through to its heart. We often start by browning the surface of the food lightly, then adding liquid before covering it with a lid. Not all my pans have a lid. I have to use a plate sometimes.

A lid also permits the food to cook in its own steam. Mussels and clams, perhaps, things that produce their own juices and take just seconds to cook. We trap in the steam they produce, encouraging them to cook more quickly. Sometimes, the lid is on tight, so no steam escapes; other times it is left at a jaunty angle, like a cap.

I have an assortment of hob pans, some of which have been around as long as my oldest friends: a cast iron pan, whose thick base allows a lump of meat to cook evenly; a set of stainless steel pans that I have had for two decades (the best money I have ever spent); a copper-based sauté pan with curved edges and a lid, for cooking chicken pieces; and a vast pan with tall sides that gives room for pasta to roll around in deep boiling water. Not many, I concede, but that is generally all I need.

Cooking on the hob is often about heat control – the first burst of heat to form a crust, then a lower heat to cook the meat, fish or vegetable right through to the middle. If we turn the heat down really low, or use a diffuser mat, then the food can be left unattended. Generally, anything cooked on the hob needs watching, even if it is only to give it the occasional stir. I have burned many a pot of soup (and, incessantly, chickpeas) by being distracted. It takes a while to get to know the intricacies of a gas or electric hob.

I tend to think of the hob as the home of the cheap dinner. Less expensive to heat than the oven, the hob is where we can make a bowl of pasta, a hearty main-course soup, a noodle broth or a vast pan of mussels. This is the place I boil lentils for a bolognaise, poach a chicken for salad or cook up a mound of mash for sausages. What I like about cooking on the hob is that I can stir to my heart's content. Unlike opening the oven door, grabbing a tea towel and sliding out the baking dish, you simply have to lift the lid and you are immediately in touch with your food. This is the food whose smell fills our kitchen as we cook. It brings us to the table. The joy of stirring a dish while we drink and chat with those we are feeding. Cooking on the hob allows us to get closer to our cooking than roasting or baking. It allows us a sniff, a peep, a stir, a taste. The very best sort of hands-on cooking.

A few favourite hob-top dinners

Cannellini mash, butter and spices, warm naan
Warm and mash cannellini (or haricot) beans. Toast some whole cumin seed, ground coriander and ground chilli in a pan till fragrant, then add to the beans. Stir a little melted butter into the bean mash, then scoop up with warm naan bread. Or serve in a soft mound alongside grilled gammon or grilled lamb cutlets.

A chicken stroganoff, of sorts
Cut brown and white chicken meat into rough chunks (about the size of a walnut in its shell), then roll them in a mixture of ground paprika, salt and pepper. Heat a little butter and oil in a shallow pan, add a sliced onion and let it soften. Add a handful of quartered small mushrooms and let both lightly brown, then tip out into a bowl. Add a little more butter to the pan. When it froths, add the chicken and let it colour. Tip the onion and mushroom in with the chicken, stir in a generous seasoning of Dijon mustard, salt and pepper, then add a pot of crème fraîche. Simmer for 6–7 minutes. Eat with noodles, bread or rice.

A few thoughts

- You could spread the bean mixture on to bruschetta or crispbread and place the crisp bacon, cut into short lengths, on top.
- Once you have rinsed the beans, you can cook them in water or a little olive oil, depending how rich you want the mash to be.
- Canned butter beans and cannellini seem to make the smoothest mash. Chickpeas produce a slightly grainy texture.
- If you drain a can of beans, warm them in a little olive oil and then blitz to a smooth mash, you have an instant dip for scooping up with chunks of torn baguette or toasted sourdough.

Creamed beans, garlic bread, olive oil

Drain a couple of cans of butter beans, chickpeas or cannellini beans, rinse them in a colander under cold running water, then put them in a saucepan with a can of water and bring to the boil. Lower the heat and simmer for 10 minutes to heat thoroughly, then drain. Mash with a potato masher or fork, or in a food processor, beating in a couple of tablespoons of olive oil and seasoning with salt, black pepper and lemon juice. Mash a clove of garlic with a little butter, spread it on hot toast or a halved baguette, then spread generously with the bean mash. Trickle over some more olive oil, perhaps something rich and fruity.

Flageolet, green herbs, olive oil

Rinse a couple of cans of flageolet (or cannellini) beans, put them in a saucepan with 2 tablespoons of olive oil and some salt and pepper and warm them for a few minutes. Roughly mash the beans with a fork or potato masher, then pile on to slices of toasted baguette and scatter with chopped parsley, basil and a few capers. Trickle over a little olive oil and finish with a grinding of pepper.

Bacon and Beans

smoked bacon, chickpeas, butter beans, onion,
garlic, paprika, crème fraîche

Peel **a medium onion** and roughly chop it. Warm **a film of olive oil**
in a deep frying pan and soften the onion in it over a moderate heat.
Peel and crush **a large clove of garlic** and add to the pan. Drain
a 400g can of chickpeas and **a 400g can of butter beans** and rinse
briefly in a colander under running water. Put them in a pan with
2 tablespoons of oil and heat for 5 minutes to warm thoroughly.
Add to the cooked onion.

Season the onion and beans with **a little ground paprika** and some
salt and black pepper. Blitz in a food processor, then stir in **a couple
of tablespoons of crème fraîche**. Grill or fry **8 rashers of smoked
streaky bacon** till thoroughly crisp. Serve with the bean purée.

For 2, as a light meal. The soft earthiness of mashed beans. The
warmth of spice. Crisp bacon.

177

Chicken Skin Popcorn

chicken skin, popping corn, butter, rosemary

Set the oven at 180°C/Gas 4. Remove the skin from **4 free-range chicken thighs** with a small knife, place it flat on a baking sheet, then lightly season with coarse sea salt and black pepper. Bake for 20–25 minutes till crisp and golden. Remove from the oven and place on a piece of kitchen paper to fully crisp.

Melt **50g butter** in a small pan, add **a heaped tablespoon of rosemary needles**, very finely chopped, and cook very briefly till fragrant.

Crumble the chicken skin into small pieces and season generously with sea salt. (Only you know how salty you like your popcorn, but start with half a tablespoon of sea salt flakes.)

Melt a further **30g butter** in a deep pan. Add **150g popping corn** and cover with a lid. Over a medium heat, cook the corn till it starts to pop, shaking the pan vigorously from time to time to ensure it doesn't scorch.

As soon as all the corn has popped – there may be a few stubborn kernels that refuse – pour in the melted rosemary butter and add the crumbled chicken skin.

For 4, as a snack. Scandalously salty, moreish popcorn.

A thought

I use a thick, semi-soft chorizo for this. A firm one might need to be quite thinly sliced to stop it becoming chewy during its short time in the pan. I also go for a hot one, so good with the clam juices, but there are plenty of mild chorizo around if you prefer. Picante is the spicy one, dulce the sweeter.

Sweet mussels, crisp smoked bacon

Cut 200g smoked bacon into large dice and fry it in a shallow pan. As it starts to crisp and the fat turns amber, add 750g small, sweet mussels in their shells. Toss together, allowing the bacon and mussel juices to mix. Add a glass of vermouth, such as Noilly Prat, and a handful of chopped flat-leaf parsley.

Mackerel wrapped in bacon

Season fillets of fresh mackerel with black pepper and twist a rasher, or even two, of smoked streaky bacon around each one. Cook under an overhead grill till the mackerel is tender and the bacon is crisp. Eat with a salad of thinly sliced fennel, dill and lemon juice.

Pancetta, salmon, crisp baguette

Cut thin slices of pancetta into postage-stamp-sized pieces and fry in a non-stick pan for a couple of minutes. Add chunks of cold cooked salmon and leave to cook, with the occasional shake of the pan to stop them sticking. Try not to let the salmon break up. Split pieces of crisp baguette open and slather with mayonnaise. Pile the salmon and pancetta on top of the mayo and squeeze over a little lemon juice.

Mussels with Clams and Chorizo

mussels, clams, chorizo, dry sherry

Wash **500g mussels** and **500g clams**, discarding any with cracked or broken shells, any that seem lifeless or exceptionally light, and any open ones that refuse to close when tapped on the side of the kitchen sink. Tug off any wiry beards from the mussels and knock off any barnacles with the back of a knife.

Remove the skin from **200g chorizo** and slice or tear it into small chunks. Get a wok or frying pan very hot, add **a tablespoon of oil**, then add the chorizo and let it colour lightly, tossing it around the pan so it doesn't burn. Pour in **a glass of dry sherry** and let it boil briefly (you need the flavour, not the alcohol), then put the washed mussels and clams into the pan and let them cook for a minute or two, till the shells open, discarding any that stubbornly refuse to open. Season lightly.

Serve immediately, with the juices and some bread for mopping them up.

For 2. Shellfish, sherry and sausages.

Any ribbon pasta will be fine for serving with the lentil ragù, as will almost any smaller shape that will hold some sauce, especially orecchiette.

Lentils and golden onions, smoked bacon, crème fraîche

Cook Puy lentils in boiling water until tender and then drain. Cook a thinly sliced onion in a little olive oil or butter till pale gold, then add 4 chopped smoked bacon rashers and cook till they are sizzling and the onion is a rich golden colour. Stir in the drained lentils, some roughly chopped parsley and couple of tablespoons of crème fraîche. Eat with steamed brown rice, with pasta or as a side dish.

Lentils, green peas and grilled salmon

Boil Puy lentils, drain them and toss with warm cooked broad beans, popped from their grey skins, some cooked peas and finely sliced spring onions. Stir through a generous glug or two of olive oil, then add large pieces of crumbled grilled salmon. Maybe serve as a side dish.

Goat's cheese, lentils, olive oil

Simmer Puy lentils in vegetable stock until tender, then drain. Toss with a little olive oil, salt and pepper. Serve warm, topped with thick slices cut from a log of English goat's cheese, such as Tymsboro, Ragstone or Dorstone. Or use the cooked lentils as a base on which to pile feta cheese that you have baked in foil with thyme leaves and a little olive oil.

Lentil Bolognaise

Puy lentils, carrots, onion, vegetable stock,
crème fraîche, balsamic vinegar, pappardelle

Cut **2 carrots** into small dice, peeling them if you wish, then leave them
to cook over a moderate heat in **3 tablespoons of olive oil** in a deep pan.
Peel and finely slice **an onion**, add to the pan and cook for a good
15 minutes, till the onion is deep gold and the carrots lightly browned.

Tip **200g Puy lentils**, rinsed if necessary, into the pan, then pour in
a litre of vegetable stock and bring to the boil. Lower the heat so the
liquid simmers and leave to cook until the lentils are soft – anything
from 25–40 minutes. Season with salt towards the end of cooking.

Put a large pan of water on to boil for the pasta and salt it
generously. Cook **300g pappardelle** in it until *al dente*.

While the pasta cooks, remove half the lentils and their liquid and
blitz to a rough purée in a blender or food processor. Return them to the
pan and stir. Mix in **2 tablespoons of crème fraîche** and **a tablespoon of
balsamic vinegar** and check the seasoning. Bring almost to the boil.

Drain the pasta, divide between warm bowls, then spoon over the
lentil ragù.

For 4. Earthy, frugal and filling.

A change

Chopped tarragon, mint and chervil are the most appropriate herbs to add. A scattering of grated Parmesan, tiny nuggets of pecorino or shavings of aged ricotta will add a savoury hit. Shelled peas, mangetout or snow peas will bring more sweetness, just as sliced button mushrooms cooked in a little butter will introduce an earthy quality. The recipe is a gentle one, so it is not worth adding anything too robust or powerful.

Other delicate summer flavours for pasta

- Fold lightly cooked green beans into cooked ribbon pasta with some crème fraîche, Parmesan and a little grated lemon zest.
- Warm double cream in a small pan, add black pepper, flaked cooked salmon and chopped dill. Toss with pasta.
- Boil and drain shelled or frozen peas, toss them with small pasta, watercress, basil and warmed crème fraîche.
- Drain preserved artichokes from their oil, slice them, then warm with torn parsley, lemon juice and shredded Parma ham. Toss with any ribbon pasta.
- Chop a couple of handfuls of mixed fresh herbs – basil, tarragon, dill, parsley, chives. Mash them into softened butter with a little salt and black pepper. Drain the cooked pasta – ribbons of fettuccine or pappardelle would be appropriate – then toss with the soft, but not melted, butter.

Orecchiette with Ricotta and Broad Beans

orecchiette, ricotta, broad beans

Drop **400g broad beans** into boiling, lightly salted water, cook for 7–8 minutes, depending on their size, then drain in a colander. Cook **250g orecchiette or other medium-sized pasta** in deep, generously salted boiling water until *al dente*. Whilst the pasta is cooking, squeeze the beans from their grey skins. Discard the skins and toss the beans in **a splash of olive oil**.

Drain the pasta, tip into a large bowl, then add the broad beans. Stir **a couple of tablespoons of olive oil** into **200g ricotta** – there may be a little curdling – and season with black pepper. Drop large spoonfuls of the ricotta on top of the pasta and serve.

For 3. Delicate flavours. The marriage of warm and cool.

Liver and bacon ragù. Amazing depth from a ragù so quickly cooked. The richness of liver

Dice 8 thick rashers of smoked streaky bacon and cook over a low to moderate heat in a non-stick pan. Peel and dice a red onion. As the bacon fat starts to run, add the onion to the pan and cook for 5 minutes. Finely chop 6 chestnut mushrooms, stir them into the bacon and onion and continue cooking till the mushrooms are glossy and tender. Push everything to one side of the pan, add 250g lamb's liver, chopped into small dice, and cook for 2–3 minutes. Cut 12 cherry tomatoes into quarters and stir them in. Let the tomatoes cook down for a few minutes, then add a wine glass or so of stock. Leave to simmer for 5–10 minutes, scraping any goodies stuck to the base of the pan into the sauce, until the sauce has reduced a little – it won't thicken a great deal.

Cook 125g fettuccine in generously salted boiling water. Drain the pasta and toss gently with the sauce.

A vegetable version. Ragù of leek and Caerphilly

Trim 2 large leeks and slice them lengthways into long, thin ribbons, like pappardelle. Cook them slowly in butter, without letting them colour, till they are soft. Add a couple of cloves of finely sliced garlic, a tablespoon of chopped tarragon, a little double cream and 150g deeply flavoured, crumbled farmhouse Caerphilly. Toss with cooked ribbon pasta. Shave a further 100g Caerphilly or so on top.

A Light Chicken Ragù

chicken, garlic, spring onion, lemon thyme,
parsley, lemon, chicken stock, pappardelle or
fettuccine

Cut **400g boned chicken breast** into very small dice, just a step or two
up from mince. Peel and thinly slice **2 cloves of garlic** and thinly slice
a spring onion. Lightly brown the chicken in **a little oil or butter.** As
the colour turns, add the garlic and spring onion. Stir in **a tablespoon
of lemon thyme, 2 tablespoons of chopped parsley**, some salt and
pepper, then **2 tablespoons of plain flour.** Cook for a minute or two,
then pour in **400ml hot chicken stock.** Simmer for 15 minutes, stirring
regularly. Check the seasoning and finish with **a squeeze of lemon.**

Cook **125g pappardelle or fettuccine** in deep, generously salted water,
then drain and toss with the ragù sauce.

For 2. Light, creamy and fresh. A change from a dark ragù sauce.

With prosciutto, crème fraîche and tarragon

Sauté 2 large boned chicken breasts in a little olive oil over a low to moderate heat, turning them regularly and basting them as they cook. Remove them from the pan as soon as their juices run clear when you pierce the meat with a skewer at the thickest part. Tear 4 thin slices of prosciutto into pieces and roughly chop a handful of tarragon leaves. Add a little butter to the pan, followed by the prosciutto and tarragon, then stir in a couple of tablespoons of crème fraîche and return the chicken and any juices to the pan. Green beans would be good with this. For 2.

With tomato sauce and mozzarella

Slice a couple of cloves of garlic, warm them in olive oil, then add a can of chopped tomatoes, a handful of torn basil leaves and a little salt and black pepper. Simmer for 6–7 minutes. Brown 4 chicken breasts in a little oil, then place in a baking dish, pour over the tomato and basil sauce and lay thick slices of mozzarella on top. Scatter over a layer of grated Parmesan and bake for 25 minutes at 180°C/Gas 4. For 4.

Chicken, earthy spice, sweet sharp apricots

Brown 6 chicken thighs in oil in a deep pan, then add a peeled and finely sliced onion and a couple of sliced cloves of garlic, followed by 2 tablespoons of ras el hanout. Add a handful of dried apricots, 2 chopped tomatoes and 800ml chicken stock. Bring to the boil, season and cover with a lid, then simmer gently for a good hour. For 3.

Ras el Hanout
Chicken and Spelt

chicken wings, pearled spelt, ras el hanout,
cabbage, butter

Fry **8 chicken wings** in **3 tablespoons of oil** in a casserole. When
they start to brown, stir in **2 tablespoons of ras el hanout**. Add
200g pearled spelt and pour in 400ml boiling water from the kettle.
Bring back to the boil, lid on, then transfer to an oven heated to
180°C/Gas 4 and bake for 35–40 minutes, till the liquid has been
absorbed.

Shred **4 cabbage leaves**, add them to the casserole with **30g butter**
and cook briefly on the hob before serving.

Enough for 2–3. Tender grains. The warmth of Moroccan spice.

Smoked haddock, the cosseting of mushrooms and cream

Thinly slice a handful of button mushrooms and cook them in a shallow non-stick pan with a little butter till they are soft and lightly coloured. Stir in a drained and rinsed 400g can of cannellini beans and warm through, stirring from time to time. Put a couple of pieces of smoked haddock fillet, about 200g each, into a second pan, with 400ml double cream. Add a couple of bay leaves and 6 black peppercorns and simmer gently for about 12 minutes, until the fish is tender. Lift the fish out on to plates. Pour the cream through a sieve on to the beans and mushrooms, cook briefly (some chopped parsley would be good, if you have it), then spoon the mixture over the fish.

Kippers, butter beans and cream

Put a couple of kipper fillets in a shallow pan. Pour over enough double cream just to cover them, add 6 black peppercorns and a bay leaf and bring to the boil. Immediately turn down the heat. Let the cream simmer gently for 10 minutes, then turn off the heat. Cover the pan with a plate and give the cream 10 minutes more to infuse with smoke from the kippers, bay and pepper. Empty a 400g can of butter beans into a sieve and rinse them under cold running water. Break the fish into large bite-sized pieces, removing the bones as you go. Warm the beans over a moderate heat with enough of the cream to cover them. Add the pieces of kipper, a little salt, lemon juice and, if you like, a grating of horseradish.

Smoked Haddock
with Lentils

smoked haddock, green lentils, carrots, onion,
vegetable stock, double cream, parsley, bay,
black peppercorns

Put **250ml double cream** in a shallow pan. Remove the skin from
a piece of smoked haddock weighing about 350g and add the haddock
to the pan. Add **6 black peppercorns** and **3 bay leaves**, bring to the
boil, then turn off the heat and cover with a lid. The fish will cook in
the residual heat.

Finely dice **a couple of medium carrots** and **an onion**. Cook them
in **a thick slice of butter** over a moderate heat for 5 minutes, then add
150g green lentils and **400ml vegetable stock**. Bring to the boil and
turn the heat down to a simmer. Leave to cook for 20 minutes, till
the lentils are approaching softness, then stir in the cream from the
fish. Continue cooking, letting the liquid reduce until it just covers
the lentils.

Add **a good handful of chopped parsley** and season carefully with
salt and pepper. Divide between 2 dishes, putting the haddock on top
of the lentils.

For 2. The calming quality of smoked fish and cream.

A thought

Whole smoked mackerel is moister and more creamy fleshed than the fillets. But use whatever you can. I like to keep the pieces of fish large and heat them gently in the cream with as little stirring as possible, so as not to crush them.

For a change

- The cream can be infused with other flavours, such as a few sprigs of thyme or a tablespoon or two of chopped dill, tarragon or chervil. Mustard is a fine addition, especially the grainy sort. A little lemon is good too.
- You could add lightly sautéed strips of courgette in place of the green beans in the recipe opposite.

Green spinach, smoked mackerel, ribbons of pasta

Cook the mackerel in the cream as opposite. Boil enough pappardelle for 2 in deep, salted water. Wash 4 handfuls of spinach and, without shaking dry, put them into a pan with a lid. Cover and let the leaves steam briefly till they have just wilted, then drain in a colander and rinse under cold running water. Squeeze dry with your hands, then tuck bits of spinach between ribbons of pasta and shards of torn smoked mackerel. Pour over the seasoned cream.

Chewy, glossy bagel. Creamy smoked fish

Break a smoked mackerel fillet into pieces, mash it roughly with a fork, then fold in a little grain mustard, black pepper and cream. Spread it on to bagels, with or without slices of cucumber.

Smoked Mackerel
and Green Beans

smoked mackerel, green beans, double cream,
bay, parsley

Pour **450ml double cream** into a saucepan, season with coarsely ground
black pepper and add **a couple of bay leaves**. Place over a moderate
heat. Once the cream is almost at the boil, break **350g smoked mackerel**
into large pieces and drop into the cream. Simmer for a couple of
minutes, then turn off the heat. During this time the cream will soak up
the smoky flavours of the mackerel.

Top and tail **250g green beans** and blanch them in salted water. Drain
the beans and toss with the cream and mackerel. Warm gently, season
thoughtfully and serve with **a little chopped parsley**.

Enough for 2. The ever-useful smoked mackerel.

A few thoughts

- Basically Spanish-inspired scrambled eggs, this is a dish to which you could add cooked prawns, bacon or ham, or chopped cooked greens such as spinach or summer cabbage.
- Chopped or quartered mushrooms can be added to the pan before the spice paste, as can morcilla, peppers, chorizo or slices of squid. It is very much a recipe for last-minute inspiration.

Asparagus and prawns

Sizzle butter in a pan, drop in some shavings of asparagus (I use a vegetable peeler), let them soften for a minute, then add a handful of prawns. As soon as they are hot, stir in the eggs. If you have some, a handful of tarragon would be good.

A salsa scramble

Sizzle a finely chopped tomato, a little finely chopped chilli and some chopped spring onion in a little butter, then stir in half a chopped avocado, a squeeze of lime juice and a little coriander. Use half as the base of the scramble, adding the eggs to it once it is hot. Serve the other half as a salsa on the side.

A bacon scramble

Sizzle chopped bacon in butter, then add a handful of croutons and fry till crisp. Pour in lightly beaten eggs, add a handful of chopped parsley and scramble as opposite.

Spinach and Parmesan

Steam a couple of large handfuls of spinach and chop roughly, then stir into the beaten eggs together with finely ground black pepper and a couple of tablespoons of Parmesan or Grana Padano cheese. Add to the melted butter, stirring as opposite to give a loose scramble.

Spiced Scrambled Eggs

eggs, curry powder, cumin seeds, dried chilli,
tomato, spring onions, coriander

In a food processor, blitz **a large tomato** with **a teaspoon each of
decent curry powder, cumin seeds** and **dried chilli flakes**. Put the
resulting paste into a shallow pan with **a little butter** and fry gently
over a moderate heat for 4 or 5 minutes, stirring regularly. Finely slice
2 spring onions and add them to the spice paste. Break **5 eggs**
straight into the pan and stir quickly so that they scramble and mix
with the spiced tomato paste and **a little coriander**. This dish is all
about speed, so make it quickly and get everyone to the table first. It
needs to be eaten fresh from the pan. For 2.

Gorgonzola, pasta, a little olive oil

Cook any pasta in deep, boiling, generously salted water. Warm ripe
Gorgonzola in a small bowl over hot water, stir in a little cream and
olive oil. Drain the pasta, then toss with the melted cheese sauce.

Courgette and lemon pasta

Dice a couple of medium-sized courgettes, then cook the cubes in
butter in a shallow pan till they are tender and golden. Finely chop
2 large garlic cloves and let them colour with the courgettes. Add a
handful of chopped mint leaves, a little grated lemon zest and a little
more butter. Cook enough small pasta, such as penne or rigatoni,
for 2 in deep, salted boiling water, drain and toss with the courgette
and lemon.

Basil Tomato Pasta

basil, tomatoes, pasta, olive oil

Cook **150g conchiglie or other pasta** in deep, salted water till just tender. Make a dressing by putting **150ml olive oil, 20g basil leaves, a beefsteak tomato** and a little salt and pepper into a food processor or blender and blitzing till you have a rough dressing. Drain the pasta and return to the pan, then add the dressing and toss gently.

For 2. Hot pasta. Cold, fragrant dressing.

A few thoughts

- Wet potato will give a sloppy mash. Steaming the potatoes in their skins instead of boiling them is a successful way to get a dry, fluffy mash.
- For extra-light mashed potatoes, whip the mixture further after mashing, using a wooden spoon or an electric beater.
- Colcannon, an Irish recipe from the bubble and squeak family, is traditionally served unfried, with kale, potatoes and milk as the main ingredients. Often eaten with boiled ham, it can be a sound use for leftover ham too, tearing it up and mixing it with the mashed potato, as opposite.
- Use crème fraîche instead of milk, or add a handful of grated cheese.
- Fry the mixture in a little butter or bake till nicely browned, if you prefer, but don't call it colcannon if you do.

Cheese and onion mash

In the colcannon recipe opposite, substitute spring onions for the leeks. In place of ham, fold in cubes of Taleggio, Camembert or other soft cheese, leaving it to soften in the warm potato. You will need about 100g cheese to 350g of cooked potato.

Rumbledethumps, as robustly delicious as it sounds

Fry sliced onions in butter and a little oil till they are soft, deep gold and glossy. This will take a good 20 minutes, if not longer. Stir them into the mashed potato with shredded cooked cabbage, then pile into a dish and brown lightly in the oven.

Bubble cakes

Take the colcannon opposite and pat the mixture into small cakes. Toss them lightly in flour, then fry in butter and oil till a crisp crust has appeared underneath. Turn them tenderly and cook the other side. Serve on their own or with a fried egg on top.

Ham and Kale Colcannon

ham, kale, potatoes, leeks, milk

Peel **500g large, floury potatoes**, cut them into large chunks and cook in boiling water. Slice **250g leeks** and fry in **butter**, till soft but not coloured. Steam **a couple of handfuls of kale** and drain. When the potatoes are soft enough to mash, drain, then beat to a fluff either with a potato masher and a wooden spoon or in a food mixer. Beat in about **150ml hot milk** and **a thick slice of butter**.

Tear up about **250g thick-cut cooked ham**, chop the kale and fold them into the potato, together with the cooked leeks. Season with salt and black pepper and serve.

For 3–4. Comfort food of the highest order.

Mackerel with Bulgur
and Tomato

mackerel, bulgur, tomatoes, vegetable stock,
red wine vinegar

Heat **400ml vegetable stock** in a saucepan, then pour it over
150g bulgur wheat and set aside for 15 minutes or so, until most of
the liquid has been absorbed by the grain.

Halve **8 medium-sized tomatoes** and cook them under an
overhead grill till soft and the skins have started to blacken. Remove
the skins, pour in **a tablespoon of red wine vinegar** and season with
black pepper. Crush the tomatoes with a fork to give a thick, roughly
textured sauce and keep warm.

Brush **4 mackerel fillets** with **a little oil**, season with salt and
pepper, then cook under an overhead grill for a few minutes, skin-
side down, till the fish is opaque and a flake will pull away from the
skin. I like to turn the fillets skin-side up for a minute or so, to crisp
them lightly. Divide the bulgur between 2 plates, add the mackerel
fillets, then spoon over the grilled tomato sauce.

For 2. Homely grain. The sweet sharp joy of tomatoes.

A few thoughts

- Use another type of fish if you prefer.
- You could peel the potatoes before cooking them and mash them to a soft cream for a more classic result.
- Include a little cooked spinach, well drained and squeezed dry, in place of the leeks.
- Add a few capers.
- Make a hollandaise to accompany.

Kipper, courgette, dill

To the basic potato mixture opposite, add cooked and lightly crushed kippers (keep the pieces quite large) and some shredded courgette that you have briefly fried with a little butter and dill. Fold into the potato mixture, shape and fry.

Smoked Haddock and Leek Cakes

smoked haddock, leeks, potatoes, milk, bay,
black peppercorns

Scrub **400g King Edward or other floury baking potatoes** then cut
into large chunks. Boil in a deep pan of salted water for 10–15
minutes, till tender enough to mash. Drain the potatoes and crush
them with a potato masher or a fork, keeping the texture rough and
lumpy. Finely shred **400g leeks**, then let them completely soften in
a thin slice of butter over a moderate heat.

Place **300g smoked haddock, 250ml milk, a bay leaf** and **6 black
peppercorns** in a pan. Bring the milk to the boil, turn off the heat,
cover with a lid and leave for 10 minutes, until opaque (this is all the
cooking it needs). When the fish is opaque, remove, discard the skin
and break the flesh into large flakes, then mix with the crushed
potatoes and half the cooked leeks. Shape into 6 rough patties, then
fry in **a little oil and butter** till crisp and golden and serve with the
remaining leeks.

Makes 6. Enough for 3. A modern rough-textured take on the
classic fish cake.

Brown Shrimps, Linguine, Dill

brown shrimps, linguine, dill, garlic,
vermouth, lemon

Put a large pan of water on to boil, then salt it generously. When the
water boils, add **200g linguine**. Cook for the time given on the
packet, about 8 minutes.

Peel and crush **2 medium cloves of garlic**. Put **5 tablespoons of oil** in
a small pan, add the garlic and fry briefly till soft, then add **200g brown
shrimps** and **a large handful of chopped dill**. Season with black
pepper, salt and the **grated zest and juice of a lemon** and **a tablespoon
of Noilly Prat or other vermouth**. Bring to the boil then remove from
the heat.

Drain the linguine, tip in the shrimp mixture and toss them gently
together.

For 2. Light lunch. Summer flavours. The fun of little shrimps
and dill.

A few thoughts

Chop and change the vegetables to suit what you have available. The point is to keep the ingredients fresh and green. French beans, chopped into short pieces, are an option, as is thickly shredded, mild-tasting spring cabbage.

To make the soup more substantial, you could add spaghetti, broken into short lengths, or any of the tiny star- or rice-shaped pastas. As this is a variation on the traditional tomato-based minestrone, there are no rules. You can add and subtract according to what is in your shopping bag. You could include some bits of chopped pancetta too. Cook them with the leeks and onions.

A cream of cauliflower soup with mussels

Wash and thoroughly inspect 800g mussels, discarding any that are open and refuse to close when tapped hard on the side of the sink or have broken shells. Put the mussels in a pan with 6 peppercorns, a couple of bay leaves and 200ml of water. Bring to the boil, cover with a lid, and steam for a couple of minutes till all the shells have opened. Discard any that remain closed.

Remove the mussels from the pan, leaving the cooking liquid inside. Pick the mussels out of their shells and place in a bowl.

Break a medium cauliflower into large florets and steam over the mussel cooking liquid for 10–15 minutes, till tender, then strain the cooking liquid.

Toast 2 tablespoons of hazelnuts in a frying pan, till golden. Blitz the cauliflower and the strained mussel liquor in a blender or food processor till smooth. Stir in 225ml double cream then check the seasoning and reheat if necessary (probably not). Add the shelled mussels, some chopped parsley and the toasted hazelnuts. For 3–4.

A Quick(ish) Green Minestrone

broad beans, baby leeks, spring onions,
courgettes, flageolet beans, peas, vegetable
stock, chives, parsley, Parmesan

Pod **400g broad beans**, boil them in lightly salted water, then drain
and cool under running water. Unless they are really young and
small, I like to pop them out of their pale skins, but it is up to you.

Thickly slice **200g leeks** (I like to do them diagonally), then thinly
slice **2 spring onions**. Place them in a saucepan, with **a couple of
tablespoons of olive oil**, and cook gently, covered with a piece of
greaseproof or baking parchment. The parchment will encourage
them to steam and soften rather than fry. You want them to be tender,
but they shouldn't brown. Cut **200g courgettes** into short lengths.

When the leeks and onions are soft and still bright green, remove
the paper, add the courgettes, **two 200g cans of flageolet beans**,
rinsed, **200g peas** and then **a litre of vegetable stock**, bring to the boil,
then turn down to a simmer. Add the broad beans and **10g chives**,
chopped into short lengths. Roughly chop **a handful of parsley** and
stir into the soup. Season and pass round a dish of **grated Parmesan** at
the table for those who want it. For 4–6.

Black garlic and almonds

Squeeze the soft flesh from a head of black garlic, mix to a smooth paste with a few tablespoons of olive oil, then turn the chicken fillets in it. Cook for a few minutes in a shallow non-stick frying pan. When the chicken is almost ready, toss in a handful of whole, salted Marcona almonds.

Sort-of satay

Make a loose paste with crunchy peanut butter, white wine vinegar, crushed dried chilli flakes and a little grain mustard. Spread on to the chicken and cook in a shallow non-stick pan in a little olive oil.

Paprika, Mustard Chicken Goujons

chicken fillets, smoked paprika,
Dijon mustard, breadcrumbs

Mix **3 heaped tablespoons of Dijon mustard** with **2 teaspoons of hot smoked paprika** and a little salt and pepper. Season **400g chicken fillets**. Put **25g panko or other crisp white breadcrumbs** on a plate. Press the fillets first into the mustard and paprika, then into the crumbs. Shallow-fry in **sunflower oil** till crisp, then drain briefly on kitchen paper. Serve with mayonnaise and wedges of lime.

For 2. Smoky, crunchy chicken.

Harissa Carrots

spring carrots, harissa paste, garlic, egg,
white wine vinegar, Dijon mustard

Trim the leaves of **650g spring carrots**, then blanch, whole, in a deep
pan of boiling, lightly salted water, till tender. Peel and mash **2 cloves
of garlic** with a pestle and mortar or in a blender, then blend with
**an egg yolk, 4 tablespoons of olive oil, 1 tablespoon of white wine
vinegar, 1 tablespoon of Dijon mustard** and **1–2 tablespoons of
harissa paste.**

Drain the carrots carefully and place on a serving dish. Pour over
the dressing whilst the carrots are still warm and serve with steamed
brown rice.

For 4. The sweetness of carrots. The balance of spice.

One-pan Sunday Lunch

chicken thighs, potatoes, white breadcrumbs,
double cream, milk, butter, thyme, sage,
vegetable or chicken stock

You will need a large, shallow pan for this. Heat **a little oil** in the pan
and brown **4 chicken thighs** in it over a moderate to high heat, then
remove them and set aside. Cut **400g potatoes** into large chunks and
brown them in the chicken pan, adding more oil if necessary. Return
the chicken to the pan and pour in **400ml hot vegetable or chicken
stock**. Lower the heat, cover the pan with a lid and leave to cook for
about 20 minutes.

Remove the chicken and potatoes from the pan. Pour **300ml milk**
and **100ml double cream** into the pan, scraping at the toasty, crusty
chicken bits on the base with a wooden spoon. They will flavour the
sauce. Tip in **150g soft white breadcrumbs**, add **2 tablespoons of
lemon thyme** (or just garden thyme) and **a tablespoon of chopped
sage leaves**. Season with salt and pepper, then add **40g butter** and
whisk until you have a smooth, creamy bread sauce. Pop the chicken
and potatoes back in to warm through, then serve.

For 2. Sunday lunch in a pan, for bread-sauce lovers.

Aubergine, orzo and basil

Trim and finely dice a large aubergine, then fry in olive oil till soft
and pale gold. Add a crushed clove of garlic, fry a minute or so
longer, then season with shredded basil, a little lemon juice and
some salt. Cook 150g orzo as opposite, then stir it into the aubergine.
Toss with a handful of grated Parmesan.

Roast pork, pasta

Add cooked, drained orzo to the roasting juices of a joint of roast
pork. Stir gently and serve with the pork. The pasta will soak up the
sticky juices from the pan.

A cure

Bring some homemade or good-quality bought chicken stock to the
boil. Add cooked, drained orzo, sea salt and lemon juice, then finish
with chopped mint. Cures most things for me.

Young Turnips with Mushrooms and Orzo

turnips, orzo pasta, mushrooms, shallot, rocket

Boil **100g orzo pasta** in deep salted water for about 9 minutes, till tender. Peel **a large banana shallot or small onion** and slice it finely, then fry in **a little butter or oil** till pale gold. Remove and set aside.

Slice **200g young white turnips** into rounds about the thickness of a pound coin. Slice **100g button or small chestnut mushrooms**. Fry both in **a little butter and oil** till golden brown. Return the fried shallot to the pan, then add **2 handfuls of rocket**.

Drain the cooked pasta and toss with the shallots, turnip, rocket and mushrooms.

For 2. Earthy, frugal and mild.

On the side

- A handful of lamb's lettuce.
- Steamed green beans, tossed in chopped parsley.
- Mashed potato, a pool of it so buttery it almost slides from the plate.

Hake, parsley, cream

Fry hake fillet in butter until pale gold underneath, then turn and cook the other side. Pour a small glass of white wine into the pan, add lots of chopped parsley, then double cream. Keep shaking the pan till you have a rough, impromptu sauce.

Pink fish, piquant sauce

Swap the cod opposite for salmon. Continue as in the recipe but, instead of tarragon and capers, add a tablespoon of brined green peppercorns and a little very finely chopped rosemary.

The scent of cardamom, the luxury of cream

Bring 300ml double cream to the boil, add about 10 lightly crushed cardamom pods, then remove from the heat and let it infuse. Fry fillets of gurnard in a little butter in a non-stick pan, then pour in the cardamom-infused cream through a sieve to remove the pieces of crushed spice. Finish with salt, black pepper and coriander leaves. Eat with steamed rice.

Cod with Lemon, Tarragon and Crème Fraîche

cod, lemons, tarragon, crème fraîche, capers, bay, butter, black peppercorns

Put **350g cod fillet**, cut from the thick end of the fish, into a large, shallow pan with the **juice of 2 lemons** and **40g butter**. Chop **half a small bunch of tarragon** and add to the pan with **a bay leaf** and **6 black peppercorns**. Bring to the boil, lower the heat, cover with a lid and simmer for about 10 minutes, till the fish is opaque. Remove the fish with a fish slice and keep warm.

Chop the rest of the bunch of tarragon and add it to the pan with **a teaspoon of capers** and **3 tablespoons of crème fraîche**. The crème fraîche will turn a little grainy where it meets the lemon juice. No matter. Coarsely flake the fish and spoon the sauce over it.

For 2. Soft, white, supremely citrus fish.

Aubergine and Chickpeas

aubergine, chickpeas, rosemary, garlic

Slice **a large aubergine** into thick rounds and place them in a single layer in a grill pan or on a baking sheet. Brush with **olive oil**, scatter with **a tablespoon of chopped rosemary needles**, salt, black pepper and **2 cloves of finely crushed garlic**. Cook under an overhead grill, adding **a little more oil** as necessary, for 10 minutes or so, until the aubergine is golden brown and thoroughly soft and tender. Turn each piece and allow to brown lightly on the other side.

Drain **a 400g can of chickpeas** and warm half the contents in a small saucepan with **a little olive oil**, salt and some black pepper. Blitz in a blender or food processor with half the grilled aubergine to give a soft, quite smooth purée. Fry the reserved chickpeas for a few minutes in **a little oil** in a shallow pan till hot, then stir, whole, into the aubergine and chickpea purée. Correct the seasoning then serve with the warm, grilled aubergine and some torn sesame bread.

For 2. A textural thing.

A few thoughts

Commercial curry powders vary in heat and flavour, so use one whose qualities you know and trust, or of course mix your own.

If you want a creamy sauce, mix in a couple of tablespoons of yoghurt just before you serve. Once any yoghurt is added, remove from the heat otherwise it will curdle.

For a change

Use paneer or aubergine instead of mushrooms.

Make a slower, more complex version by starting with chopped shallots and grated ginger and allowing them to soften before adding the mushrooms. Add more liquid, water or an extra can of tomatoes, and cook for longer for a gentler, more mellow result. Introduce some herbs, such as coriander and mint, at the end of the cooking time to brighten the flavour.

Spiced Mushrooms on Naan

mushrooms, curry powder, naan, canned
tomatoes, spring onions, chilli, yoghurt, mint

Warm **a few tablespoons of oil**, or **oil and a slice of butter**, in a deep
pan over a moderate heat, then add **3 chopped spring onions** and **a
finely sliced chilli**. Cook until the onion is soft then cut **200g
chestnut mushrooms** into halves or quarters depending on their size
and add them to the pan. As soon as the mushrooms start to lightly
brown, stir in **a tablespoon of your favourite curry powder**, fry briefly,
then add **a 400g can of crushed tomatoes** and their juice. Season
generously and leave to simmer for about 20 minutes, watching the
pan carefully. Serve with warm **naan**, and if you wish, **a little yoghurt**
and **chopped mint**.

For 2. The nourishment of warm bread. The heat of spice. 221

Chilli Prawns with Watermelon

large prawns, watermelon, dried chilli flakes,
fish sauce, lime, sugar, flour, mint, coriander

Mix **50g plain flour** in a bowl with **a teaspoon of dried chilli flakes**
and a grinding of black pepper. Pour **4 tablespoons of Thai or
Vietnamese fish sauce** into a bowl, stir in **a pinch of sugar** – no more
– then add **400g large, raw peeled prawns** (fresh are best; defrosted
are fine) and leave them for 15 minutes.

Heat **a thin film of oil** in a frying pan or wok, add the prawns and
fry, moving them around as they cook, for a few minutes until they are
crisp and sweet. Remove from the pan and serve with the salad below.

Peel **a large wedge of watermelon** and pick out as many of the
seeds as you can. Cut the flesh into large chunks and toss with **the
juice of a lime, a few chopped mint leaves** and **some torn coriander**.

For 2. Mouth-popping prawns. Refreshing watermelon. 223

A thought or two

Risotto is as much about texture as flavour. Ideally, it should be neither soupy nor stiff. It should slide slowly and gracefully from the wooden spoon, rather than pour off it, or have to be shaken. The creamy quality has as much to do with the rice as the stock – arborio rice and homemade chicken stock out of preference. But the desired texture can be aided by beating in a thick slice of butter with a wooden spoon at the end of the cooking time. The correct, round-grain rice, good rich stock and constant stirring will get you there.

Torn roast chicken, thyme, Parmesan

Sometimes, at the end of a long day, I am happy to stand at the hob and just stir.

Remove four double handfuls of meat from yesterday's roast chicken and tear it into small pieces. Make a classic risotto with 200g arborio rice and a litre or so of stock. As the risotto approaches its moment, stir in 2 teaspoons of chopped thyme leaves, the chicken and a handful of grated Parmesan. Finish with a slice of butter and any jelly that may have set in the chicken's roasting tin.

Risotto

arborio rice, chicken stock, shallot, pancetta,
Parmesan

Peel **a shallot** and chop finely, then cut **150g pancetta** into small dice.
Melt **a thick slice of butter** in a wide, shallow saucepan and add the
pancetta then the onion. Leave to cook until the onion is soft but not
coloured, stirring regularly so it doesn't brown. Add **300g arborio
rice**, stirring to coat the grains in the butter and pancetta fat, then
add **600–700ml hot chicken stock**, a ladle at a time, stirring almost
continuously. You will find the rice will take about 20 minutes to
cook. The consistency should be thick and creamy.

When the rice is ready, adjust the seasoning, adding a good **3 heaped
tablespoons of grated Parmesan** and a little black pepper and salt (you
may not need any salt at all) then spoon on to plates. For 4.

Roasted Vegetable Rice

red onion, aubergine, lemon, oregano,
garlic, mint, basmati rice

Finely slice **a medium-sized red onion** and place on a roasting tray in
a single layer. Slice **an aubergine** into thick 'coins' and add to the
onion, then squeeze over **the juice of a lemon** and tuck in **4 or 5 peeled
garlic cloves**. Dampen with about **4 tablespoons of olive oil**. Scatter
with **dried oregano**, then bake for 25 minutes at 180°C/Gas 4.

Cook **200g basmati rice** in **400ml water**. Drain, add **3 tablespoons
of mint** and stir in the roasted aubergine and onion.

For 3. Homely. Aromatic. The joy of vegetables.

Anchovies, olives and basil croutes, a salad for high summer

Blitz a couple of large handfuls of basil leaves with 4 tablespoons of olive oil, then warm in a frying pan. Add small chunks of torn-up ciabatta or baguette, letting them soak up the basil oil as they crisp. Toss them over a salad of marinated anchovies, black olives, red and yellow cherry tomatoes, mozzarella and Little Gem lettuce with a glug or two of olive oil.

A can of anchovies, a few ideas

A can of anchovies in oil is an endlessly useful addition to the kitchen cupboard (I can eat them straight out of the can).
• Mash the drained anchovies into butter as a quick savoury dressing for grilled lamb cutlets.
• Tuck into a soft, floury bap or piece of ciabatta with slices of tomato.
• Scrape out the insides of a baked potato, chop the drained anchovies and fold into the potato with a slice of butter and black pepper, then pile back into the potato skin and return briefly to the oven.
• Chop drained anchovies and mash them with butter and a little black pepper then spread over a leg of lamb and roast as usual.

Anchovy, Penne, Crumbs

marinated anchovies, small penne, butter,
breadcrumbs, chilli, lemon, parsley

Cook **150g mini penne pasta** in boiling water then drain.

In a large non-stick pan, cook **a couple of handfuls of dried breadcrumbs** in **a little oil**, till golden, then remove. Add **50g butter** and **a
chopped red chilli**, then, 30 seconds later, add **the juice of half
a lemon, 100g marinated anchovy fillets, a large handful of roughly
chopped parsley** and the browned breadcrumbs and drained penne.
Toss briefly.

For 2. Soft, piquant, crisp and hot.

A smoked salmon sandwich

Rye bread, the light sort, toasted and spread with mayonnaise then layered with thickly-cut smoked salmon, shatteringly crisp smoked streaky bacon, and a little crisp, heart lettuce. If you stir some chopped dill into the mayo, then all the better.

Smoked salmon scramble

Shred the salmon into thin strips, then fold it into freshly made scrambled eggs with a twist of black pepper. It's a classic.

More interesting, perhaps, is to add a few bottled green peppercorns to the egg; include chopped chives or stir in a little finely chopped cherry tomato, so the result is more like a coarse piperade.

Smoked Salmon and Green Peppercorn Macaroni

smoked salmon, macaroni, green peppercorns in brine, butter

Cook **150g macaroni** in boiling salted water. Shred **100g smoked salmon** into thin strips. Melt **50g butter** in a small pan and add **2 teaspoons of rinsed, bottled green peppercorns**. Drain the pasta in a colander and return to the pan, add the warm green peppercorn butter and, just before eating, the strips of smoked salmon.

For 2. A light lunch. Gentle, delicate and a little piquant.

Kipper Benedict

kipper fillets, egg yolks, butter, spinach,
English muffins, lemon

Put the kettle on. Put **500g kipper fillets** into a heatproof container
or pan and pour boiling water from the kettle over them. Leave for
10 minutes, till the fish will come off the bones fairly easily. Carefully
remove every small bone.

Make a hollandaise. Soften **100g butter** in a small saucepan. Put
2 egg yolks in a heatproof bowl over a pan of simmering water.
Slowly beat in the butter with a whisk, trickling it slowly into the egg
yolks. Season with **lemon juice** and salt then remove from the heat.
Give it a regular whisk to stop it separating. Briefly steam **a handful
of spinach leaves**.

Split and toast **4 English muffins** and spoon a little hollandaise on
to each. Divide the spinach and kipper pieces between the muffins,
spoon over more hollandaise and grill for a minute or two till golden,
then eat immediately.

For 2. The reworking of an old breakfast favourite.

Little stews

Stew. Slow cooking. The bringing together of compatible flavours in liquid of some sort. Rich broth, tasty liquor. Meat edging towards tenderness hour by hour. Comforting. Healing. Safe. Yes, all that and more. But we can have a stew on a weekday when time is against us, though we might have to rethink the word a little.

I make a great little stew, a fricassée, I suppose, with rabbit and tarragon, another with onions cooked till soft with black beans, and yet another with aubergines. They have all the qualities of slow-cooked food, yet mostly are made in less than an hour. In all fairness, not many use the bone-heavy, cheap cuts this method of cooking was designed for, but the essence of the stew is still there. The deep flavours, the aromatic liquid, the tender meat and vegetables. What isn't there is the hours of waiting.

Of course, nothing will quite beat the time-honoured Irish stew, left to sort itself out in a low oven for a couple of hours. But that doesn't mean we can't have a lamb shank pot-roasted with plenty of liquid and root vegetables on the table in about an hour. We can also have chicken cooked on the bone with melting vegetables, a rich broth and crisp skin.

There is much comfort in food that has been cooked in a casserole. For the most part, it is winter cooking, the food that warms our soul. Initially saddened that it could never be part of a book about fast food, I took a long, hard look at how such recipes could be worked in order to fit in with the premise of having something good on the table within an hour or so of coming home on a working day. So here they are: a lamb dish with asparagus; a creamy, piquant chicken fricassée; a casserole of red cabbage and blue cheese; and a silky vegetable stew. Quick, warming dinners for cool days.

A few favourites

Lamb, garlic, paprika and tomato

Crush 2 large, juicy cloves of garlic and mash them with 2 tablespoons of olive oil and a good pinch of salt. Add 450g cubed lamb, rolling it round until the meat is well seasoned with the paste. Peel and roughly chop a medium onion and let it soften and lightly brown in a little oil over a moderate heat. Add the meat to the pan, letting it brown here and there, tossing occasionally. Tip in two 400g cans of chopped tomatoes and half a teaspoon of smoked paprika. Leave to simmer for 25 minutes over a low heat. Just before eating, stir in about 120g young spinach leaves and a handful of chopped coriander and check the seasoning. Let the leaves wilt briefly, then eat. Thick chunks of bread are probably the most appropriate accompaniment.

Chicken, green aniseed herb, cream, a spike of tarragon vinegar

Slice 4 chicken breasts into thick strips, toss them in sizzling butter, and when golden add the leaves from 8 sprigs of tarragon, then, a minute later, 250ml double cream. Bring it to life with 2–3 teaspoons of tarragon vinegar.

Chicken thighs, golden skin, herbs, a flash of lemon
Let 4 chicken thighs, skin on and nicely seasoned, cook in a generous slice of butter in a shallow pan till their skin is crisp and golden. Pour in a glass of white wine, a medium dry Riesling perhaps, then scrape at the crusted sediment with a wooden spoon, stirring it into the bubbling wine. Finish with chopped herbs: parsley, chervil, tarragon, dill – one or two only. Stir in the juice of a lemon, and a last slice of butter, whisking it into the juices.

One thought

Not exactly a meal in minutes, this is nevertheless one of the simplest dinners possible. The preparation time is minimal.

Rabbit, asparagus, noodles, tarragon and cream. A peaceful dinner

Cut 400g boned rabbit meat into small pieces. Heat 40g butter in a shallow pan, add the rabbit and cook over a moderate heat till delicately browned in patches. Add a bunch of asparagus, cut into short lengths, and a small bunch of chopped tarragon. Pour in a glass of white vermouth or white wine and continue cooking for a few minutes, till the asparagus is tender. Boil about 250g wide ribbon pasta in salted water and drain. Add a little cream or crème fraîche to the rabbit, check the seasoning, then drop in the drained pasta and toss gently. For 2–3.

Poached rabbit with carrots and orzo. A bowl of calm

For a pure, almost humble, meal, I like to poach a couple of rabbit joints – the meaty leg or saddle – in vegetable stock with a few new season's carrots, sliced lengthways, the most diminutive new potatoes I can find, a sprig of rosemary and a couple of thyme sprigs, bay and black pepper. I let it simmer for as long as I have (30–40 minutes is about the minimum), then I scatter a couple of spoonfuls of orzo pasta into the broth. Ten minutes later, you have a blissfully calming, almost soporific dish. Check the seasoning – it usually needs quite a bit of salt – and serve in a shallow bowl.

Slow-cooked Rabbit
with Herbs

rabbit, rosemary, thyme, tarragon, onions,
wheat beer, double cream

You will need **500g rabbit, jointed by the butcher**. Peel and roughly
chop **2 onions**, then cook them in **a thick slice of butter** over a
moderate heat till they are translucent and pale gold. Season the
pieces of rabbit all over with salt and black pepper. Push the onions
to one side of the pan if there is room, or transfer them to a bowl if
not, then add the rabbit pieces to the pan. Cook for 5 minutes, till
appetisingly browned, turning as necessary, then mix the onions in.

Finely chop the needles from **2 small sprigs of rosemary** and add
to the pan with **4 thyme sprigs, a litre of wheat beer** and some salt
and pepper. Bring to the boil, then lower the heat so the liquid
continues cooking at a low simmer. Partially cover with a lid and
leave to putter away on the stove for a couple of hours, till the rabbit
is tender. The exact timing will depend on the age and provenance of
your rabbit, but it is ready when you can remove the flesh from the
bones with a decent table knife.

The liquid in the pan will still be quite thin and plentiful, so turn up
the heat for a few minutes until it has reduced by about half (this is not
a thick sauce, and will always be the sort to eat with a spoon). *continued*   239

Pour in **100ml double cream** and stir in the leaves from **4 lush sprigs of tarragon**, chopped if they are very long. Continue simmering for 5–10 minutes, then check the seasoning. For 2.

A thought

This recipe can be padded out a bit if you want a more economical version. My feeling is for mushrooms. Cook them separately, in butter. When they are sticky on the outside, transfer them to the lamb, together with their buttery, fungal juices.

Lamb, rosemary and crème fraîche

Season 450g cubed lamb, brown it in a little oil and remove from the pan. Lightly fry some roughly chopped unsmoked bacon. Add a crushed clove of garlic, a little chopped rosemary, then some vegetable stock. Return the lamb to the pan, partially cover and leave to simmer till the meat is tender. Stir in enough soured cream or crème fraîche to give thin, but richly flavoured juices.

Lamb with Asparagus

cubed lamb, asparagus, small onions,
white wine, stock, crème fraîche, chervil

Melt **40g butter** in a deep casserole, add **450g cubed lamb** (a tender
cut, such as leg or fillet) and leave it to colour lightly for a few
minutes over a moderate to high heat. Tossing it from time to time
will help it colour evenly on all sides. Remove the meat from the pan
and set aside on a plate.

Peel **250g small onions or large shallots**, keeping them whole but
halving any that are bigger than an unshelled walnut. Add them to
the casserole and let them brown lightly, tossing them occasionally
so they colour fairly evenly.

Return the lamb and any of its juices that have escaped to the pan.
Dust **2 tablespoons of plain flour** over the meat and onions and cook
for a minute or two, stirring from time to time. Turn up the heat and
pour in **150ml white wine**. Leave the wine to bubble away till reduced
by half, scraping at the crusty bits on the base of the pan with a
wooden spatula as you go. Pour in **800ml hot stock** (can be vegetable,
lamb or even chicken) and bring to the boil, then lower the heat and
leave to simmer, partly covered, for about 30 minutes, until the meat
is tender but still has plenty of bite.   *continued*   241

Slice **300g asparagus spears** into 2 or 3 short lengths and add to the pan with salt and pepper. Continue cooking for about 5 minutes, till the asparagus is tender. Stir in **200ml crème fraîche** and **a handful of chervil leaves**. Check the seasoning and serve.

For 4. Calm cooking for a spring day.

A thought

I use large free-range chicken legs for this. You could also use breasts or drumsticks.

Roast chicken, herb mayo

Roast 4 chicken thighs with olive oil, lemon, thyme and a few whole cloves of garlic in an oven set at 200°C/Gas 6. Let the skin darken and caramelise nicely. Make a herb mayonnaise, either from scratch (2 egg yolks, a squeeze of lemon, 150ml groundnut oil, 100ml olive oil) or using a good shop-bought mayo. Stir in a small handful of chopped tarragon, a few chopped basil leaves and just a couple of chopped chives. Remove the chicken meat from the bones, tear into jagged pieces, then tuck them amongst watercress and small, crisp lettuce heart leaves. Eat with French bread and the herb mayonnaise. (The garlic can be squeezed from its skin and stirred into the herb mayo, if you wish.)

Chicken and potato salad

Boil or steam 500g new potatoes, in their skins or peeled as you wish. Mix together 4 tablespoons of crème fraîche, a tablespoon of lemon juice and 2 teaspoons of Dijon mustard. Remove the meat from the bones of the 4 roasted chicken thighs above, then toss gently with the crème fraîche dressing. Drain the potatoes and cut them in half, then toss them with the chicken and dressing. Eat as it is, or stuffed into a baguette.

Chicken with Soured Cream and Gherkins

chicken legs, soured cream, gherkins, Riesling,
button mushrooms, shallots

Put **12 small shallots** in a bowl and pour boiling water from the kettle
over them. Set aside for 10 minutes to soften the skins and make
them easier to peel. Season **2 large, free-range chicken legs**, then
brown them lightly on either side in **a little butter** over a moderate
heat. Peel the shallots, add them to the pan and let them colour
nicely all over.

Halve **250g button mushrooms** and add them to the chicken and
shallots, letting them colour lightly. Thickly slice **6 gherkins**, then add
to the pan together with **500ml Riesling**. Let the wine come to the
boil, continue cooking at an enthusiastic bubble for 3 or 4 minutes,
then lower the heat to a gentle simmer.

Cook for about 20 minutes, then stir in **150ml soured cream**,
keeping the heat quite low. Allow to warm through. Check the
seasoning and serve with potatoes, noodles or rice.

For 2. Smooth and a little piquant.

A few thoughts

You can mix your own masala, toasting and grinding spices to suit
your taste, or you can use any of the ready-made spice mixes and curry
powders available. When I am in the mood, I will toast cumin seeds
and coriander, adding dried chilli and turmeric. I will use cayenne and
black pepper or occasionally a little ground clove. Often, I will finish a
dish with garam masala. But on a weekday, when I'm quickly putting
together a curry for dinner, I use my favourite curry powder.

The earthy quality of chickpeas

Chickpeas can be used to make a curry go further. A couple of cans,
drained and rinsed, can be added to the recipe opposite. Stir them
in after the tomatoes. Alternatively, cook and serve the chickpeas
separately: pour a little oil into a shallow pan, toast a teaspoon of
cumin seeds in it, then add a peeled and finely chopped onion.
Cook until soft, then add a little grated ginger, a teaspoon of ground
coriander and a pinch of turmeric. Stir in a can of drained chickpeas.
Finish with a little garam masala, salt and a squeeze of lemon juice.

Aubergines, with the brightness of tomatoes

Warm 2 tablespoons of oil in a saucepan, add a chopped onion,
cook until softened, then stir in half a teaspoon of turmeric and half
a teaspoon of garam masala, a little ground chilli and a couple of
crushed garlic cloves. Add 4 tomatoes, roughly chopped, and 2 red
chillies, then enough water to make a loose sauce. In a separate
pan, cook the aubergine as opposite, letting it colour lightly in the oil.
Stir the aubergine into the tomatoes, then continue cooking for 20
minutes. Turn the heat up to boil off any excess liquid and stir in a
handful of coriander leaves. Eat with rice.

Aubergine Curry

aubergines, onions, tomatoes, garlic, curry powder, garam masala, ginger, coriander, yoghurt

Peel **2 medium onions** and roughly chop them. Thickly slice **2 medium aubergines**. Cook the onions and aubergines in **6 tablespoons of oil** in a large, deep pan. As they soften, peel and thinly slice **2 cloves of garlic** and add to the pan with **a tablespoon of finely chopped fresh ginger**. Stir in **2 tablespoons of mild curry powder** and fry briefly. Chop **700g tomatoes**, add to the pan and leave to simmer for 25 minutes, till the curry has thickened.

Season with salt, pepper and **a tablespoon of garam masala**. Finish with **a little fresh coriander** and offer **yoghurt** at the table. Eat with steamed rice or warm flatbread.

For 4–6. Satisfying, curiously refreshing.

Black Bean and Onion Stew

black beans, pancetta, onion, rosemary,
vegetable stock, basil

Roughly chop **a large onion**. Melt **a thick slice of butter** in a deep pan
and cook the onion in it till soft and pale gold. Cut **a thick slice of
pancetta (about 100g)** into cubes and add to the onion, cooking the
pancetta till the fat becomes translucent.

Tip in **a 400g can of black or black-eyed beans**, add **a bushy
rosemary sprig, 800ml vegetable stock** then simmer for 15–20
minutes. Season generously, add **a handful of whole basil leaves**,
then serve.

For 4. Sweet. Silky. Restoring.

Squash with chilli and orange

Peel 1kg squash, cut into large cubes and steam for 15 minutes till
tender to the point of a knife. Finely chop a medium-hot red chilli
without removing the seeds. In a bowl, mix the chopped chilli, the
finely grated zest of an orange, a little salt and black pepper and
5 tablespoons of panko breadcrumbs. Toss the squash in the crumbs,
then fry in a shallow layer of oil in a non-stick pan. When the crumbs
are golden, lift out and serve. If you have a little tomato sauce
knocking around, then all the better. For 4.

For when the tomatoes are at their best

Tomatoes, artichokes, basil croutons

Set the oven to 180°C/Gas 4. Pour 7 tablespoons of olive oil into a
blender. Tear up 20g basil and add it to the oil, then blitz to a smooth
green purée. Cut 100g good crusty bread into large cubes, put in a
baking tin, then pour over the basil oil. Toss the bread till it is coated
in the basil oil, then bake for 15 minutes till lightly crisp on the
outside but still soft in the centre.

 Halve 400g juicy, perfectly-ripe tomatoes of various colours and
toss with 150g sliced, marinated artichokes (the sort they have in a
bowl at the deli counter or in jars at the supermarket). Tuck them in
amongst the hot croutons and eat whilst the croutons are still warm.
For 2.

Chicory with Grapes, Honey and Mustard

chicory, grapes, honey, grain mustard

Trim **3 heads of chicory** and cut them in half from tip to root. Halve **200g grapes** and deseed them. Melt **40g butter** in a wide, shallow pan for which you have a lid, add the chicory, cut-side down and cook over a moderate heat for 3 or 4 minutes, covered with the lid, till the underside is taking on a little colour and there is a little translucency to the leaves, then turn. Add the grapes to the pan, continue cooking briefly till they soften, then remove the chicory and grapes to a serving dish. Stir **1 tablespoon of grain mustard** and **2 tablespoons of honey** into the butter, heat for a minute or so, then pour over the chicory and grapes.

For 2. Soft, slightly bitter leaves, sweet honey. Light lunch. A side for air-dried ham.

A few thoughts

- Lamb shanks take a long time to cook, but they need minimal preparation (which is why they have found a place in this book). Just a bit of chopping and stirring, then the oven does most of the work. Choose small shanks so that they will cook in an hour and a half. Save larger ones from older animals for the weekend. It is not strictly necessary to brown the shanks before adding the stock, but if you do there will be even more flavour in the juices.
- Use large, winter carrots so they don't collapse into the cooking liquor.
- Keep the mash rough and ready.

A Provençal version

Use a light and fruity red wine instead of stock. Try adding rosemary sprigs or a strip of orange peel to the pan. Remove the root vegetables with a draining spoon and beat to a smooth and silky purée with some of the cooking liquor.

The richness of port

Use half port, half stock. Add soft prunes and a few raisins. Serve with red cabbage that you have cooked in a lidded pot with coriander seeds, red wine vinegar, a finely chopped red chilli and a little vegetable stock.

Lamb Shanks with Crushed Roots

lamb shanks, carrots, parsnips, stock, thyme

Peel **500g large carrots** and **500g parsnips** and cut into rough chunks, then brown them lightly all over in **a little olive oil** over a moderate heat in an ovenproof dish. Place **2 small lamb shanks** on top of the vegetables, pour over **500ml stock** (lamb, chicken or vegetable), tuck in **a bunch of thyme**, season with salt and pepper, then cover the dish tightly with a lid. Bake in an oven set at 180°C/Gas 4 for 1½ hours, then remove the shanks, thyme and most of the liquid to a warm place.

Using the small amount of liquid in the dish, roughly crush the roots with a potato masher or fork and serve with the shanks and the reserved juices.

For 2, generously. A hearty, untroublesome roast.

Chicken breasts, garlic, thyme, a sweet glaze of Muscat wine

Dice a little onion, carrot and celery to the size of Dolly Mixtures, then toss them in a bowl with 4 crushed cloves of garlic, the leaves from 3 or 4 bushy sprigs of thyme and a couple of glasses of sweet Muscat wine. Add 4 chicken breasts or thighs and leave to marinate for a good hour or more. Place the chicken under a hot overhead grill, 10–12cm from the heat, spooning over the marinade as it cooks. It is ready when the juices run clear when the meat is pierced with a skewer.

Crisp golden chicken skin, soft green leaves, salt flakes

Remove the skin from 2 chicken legs or 4 thighs or drumsticks. Lay it on a baking tray, season lightly, then bake or grill till crisp and deep gold. Drain on kitchen paper and break it into small pieces. Dress 2 handfuls of soft butterhead lettuce with olive oil, Dijon mustard and lemon. Generously season the crisp chicken skin with sea salt flakes, then tuck it amongst the soft leaves. French bread. Cold butter.

Cider Thighs

chicken thighs, dry cider, chestnut mushrooms,
onions, potatoes, rosemary, black peppercorns,
bay leaves

Remove and reserve the skin from **6 large chicken thighs**, then fry
the thighs in **a little oil** in a large, shallow pan. Halve **100g chestnut
mushrooms**. Peel and roughly chop **2 medium onions** and add them
to the pan together with the mushrooms. Cut **2 baking-size potatoes**
into 4 pieces each and tuck them into the pan.

Add **the leaves from 2 sprigs of rosemary, 6 whole black peppercorns**
and **a couple of bay leaves** and then pour in **750ml English dry cider**.
Bring to the boil, lower the heat and simmer for 40 minutes.

Salt and generously pepper the reserved chicken skin, then put it
under a hot grill until crisp. Using a fork, crush half the potato pieces
into the sauce, leaving the others whole. Serve the meat, sauce and
potatoes in a shallow bowl, topped with the crisped chicken skin, with a
spoon for the sauce. Lightly cooked shredded green cabbage on the side.

For 3. Crisp skin, crisp cider, plump chicken.

Blue cheese rabbit

Split and lightly toast an English muffin. Mash together some soft blue cheese (Cashel blue, Gorgonzola, Picos, Roquefort, whatever) and a few spoonfuls of butter. Spread generously on to the toasted muffin halves and grill till sizzling lightly.

Blue cheese, new potatoes

Boil new potatoes, or at least small potatoes, in deep, lightly salted water, then drain. While they are still hot, slice them in half and place in a heatproof dish. Generously crumble over blue cheese such as Stichelton or Stilton, then place under a hot grill or in the oven till the cheese has melted.

Blue cheese, figs and a baguette

Ripe figs, soft blue cheese. You have a magical marriage of flavours and textures there. Even more so if you add some roughly torn shards of slightly burned, shatteringly crisp baguette.

Stewed Red Cabbage with Blue Cheese and Apple

red cabbage, blue cheese, Cox's apples,
white wine vinegar, sourdough bread

Finely shred **250g red cabbage**. Cut **2 Cox's apples** into segments.
Warm **2 tablespoons of groundnut oil** in a deep pan, add the cabbage
and apples and cook, stirring from time to time, till the cabbage starts
to wilt and the apples have softened a little. Pour in **100ml white wine
vinegar** and let it sizzle.

Tear **a thick slice of sourdough bread** into rough croutons and fry in
a little oil or butter till golden and crisp. Drain briefly on kitchen paper.

Divide the cabbage and apple between 2 plates. Dice **175g blue
cheese** and add it to the plates, together with the sourdough croutons.

For 2. Piquant, crisp. The rich luxury of blue cheese.

Chicken with Fennel
and Leek

chicken thighs, fennel, leeks, chicken or
vegetable stock, lemon, parsley

Season **6 bone-in chicken thighs** with salt and pepper, then brown
them lightly in a shallow pan in **a little oil** and **melted butter**. Cut
2 medium-sized leeks into cork-sized lengths, wash thoroughly then
add to the pan. Separate **2 fennel bulbs** into layers then add them to
the chicken and leeks and leave to soften for about 10 minutes,
covering with a lid. Grate in the **zest from a lemon** and continue
cooking for a minute or so.

Scatter over **2 tablespoons of flour**, then cook for a few minutes
before pouring in **a litre of chicken or vegetable stock**. Bring to the
boil, season, then lower the heat to a simmer and leave to cook for
35 minutes, covered with a lid, giving the occasional stir.

Finish the dish with **the juice of the lemon** and **a handful of
chopped parsley**. We have leeks and fennel already, so just floury
potatoes, steamed in their skins, to soak up the parsley-freckled
chicken juices.

For 3. Familiar flavours. A meal to nourish.

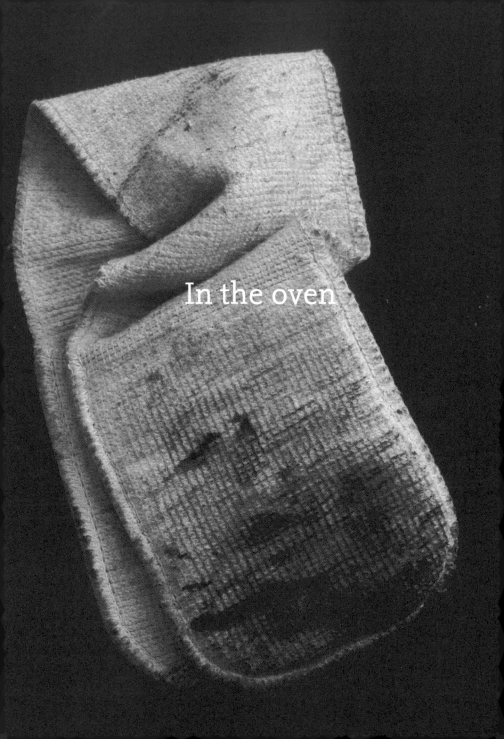

In the oven

Food cooked in the oven gets on with the job itself, without us having to watch over it. No tinkering, stirring or moving it round the pan. No having to lower the heat or prod and poke. We simply put a dish in the oven and leave it to do its stuff. That is not to say a roast won't benefit from the occasional basting with its juices, or that you can ignore a rapidly browning pie, but it does allow us time to do other things while our dinner cooks.

Many of the dishes in this section take a good half hour, even an hour or longer, in the oven. They belong in this book because their preparation time is minimal and, once they are in the oven, we are free to do something else. I like the idea of fifteen minutes of hands-on cooking followed by an hour in the oven. Anything that takes a long time both to prepare and cook is excluded.

A roasting tin is an essential piece of kit for anyone with an eye on a traditional Sunday lunch but other baking dishes are important too. A shallow dish of enamel, ovenproof china or even glass is good for a layered dish of pasta or a pie, but can also be used to bake stuffed vegetables and sausages. My enamel dishes are second hand and much loved. Pottery baking dishes can become beautifully worn with time and even heatproof glass, possibly the least romantic of all cookware, has a pleasing homeliness to it. You don't need many, maybe just a nest of enamel tins of different sizes.

The most straightforward of oven dishes, the roast chicken, has its cooking time shortened here by being cut into small joints – legs and thighs mostly – and, in one case, the bird is spatchcocked. While a whole roast chicken, with butter and thyme or lemon, could possibly fit into a book of fast food, it is probably more useful to include recipes for roast chicken pieces that take half the time of a whole bird. Here you will find baked chicken with Taleggio, a stuffed breast with smoked cheese, and spicy marmalade drumsticks. There is a quick stuffed squid whose filling of beans makes you think you are eating a dish that has been cooking for hours in a slow oven.

The essence of baking or roasting is not only its simplicity and good-natured quality but also what happens to the food. Juices leak and caramelise on the pan, edges crisp, flavours concentrate. Even roasted for a short time, chicken pieces will develop a crisp, savoury skin; the filling for a stuffed chicken breast will melt appetisingly; a belly of lamb will tenderise. But there is more. Pasta in a sauce will form a golden crust, vegetables baked in cheese sauce will turn an irresistible gold, a potato will bake to bring untold comfort.

The oven is particularly good for fish, such as sea bass and red mullet with leeks. Here, the time-heavy layered dishes such as lasagne have been shortened by replacing the ragù sauce with layers of herby sausage meat. There is also a series of little roasts, including lamb fillets with seasoned crumbs and satay drumsticks with beansprouts and curry paste. Food that needs little interference from us once the initial preparation is over. Dinner that almost cooks itself.

A few favourite oven dinners

Lime and honey
Put chicken thighs in a roasting tin, mix runny honey and lime juice to taste, season with salt and pepper, then pour over the chicken. Turn skin-side up, then roast in an oven set at 200°C/Gas 6 till the skin is golden and the juices run clear. Salt generously as you eat.

Pork with apples and maple syrup
Roughly chop a couple of apples, discarding the cores. Peel and roughly chop an onion. Mix the two then roast in a little oil in an oven set at 200°C/Gas 6 for 15 minutes. Season a pork tenderloin with salt, pepper and fennel seeds, then seal in a pan with hot oil. Add the pork to the roasting tin, trickle over maple syrup and roast for about 30 minutes depending on the weight, then leave to rest.

Soy chicken. Oh so sticky
Mix 150ml oyster sauce, 2 tablespoons of soy sauce, 2 tablespoons of light muscovado sugar, half a teaspoon of chilli flakes, 2 chopped spring onions and 2 chopped garlic cloves. Put 4 chicken pieces into a baking dish, pour in the sauce and toss gently to coat. Bake at 200°C/Gas 6 for 20 minutes, baste with the sauce, then cook for another 15–20 minutes, keeping an eye on it – it burns easily. Serve with beansprouts, crisp lettuce or watercress. For 2.

Potatoes with Spices and Spinach

potatoes, cayenne, dried chilli flakes, turmeric,
cumin, garlic, spinach, banana shallots, yoghurt,
coriander

Cut **800g large floury potatoes** into large pieces and cook in deep,
salted water for about 15 minutes, till approaching tenderness. Peel
5 banana shallots and halve them lengthways. Drain the potatoes, then
put them in a bowl, add the shallots and toss with **half a teaspoon of
cayenne, a teaspoon of dried chilli flakes, a teaspoon of crushed garlic**
and **a teaspoon each of ground cumin and turmeric.** Add **2 teaspoons
of sea salt flakes** and **4 tablespoons of groundnut oil,** then tip into a
roasting tin and bake at 200°C/Gas 6 until crisp. Wash **a couple of large
handfuls of spinach.** Put them in a pan over a moderate heat, cover
with a lid and leave for a minute or two to wilt. Toss with the crisp
potatoes and a **little yoghurt** and **torn coriander.**

Enough for 2–3. Hot, cool, crisp, soft.

Rust-red chorizo, green leaves

In the recipe opposite, substitute about 400g chorizo for the bacon. Flat-leaf parsley, coarsely chopped, is pleasing to find in the stock.

Earthy, beefy porcini, the zing of lemon

Pour a kettle of boiling water over about 10g porcini and let them soak for 10 minutes. When they are soft, layer them with the potatoes. Add the juice of half a lemon and a handful of parsley to the stock. You could use the porcini soaking water for some of the stock to bring a deep, miso quality to the dish.

Golden swede, green dill and a little fish

Peel and slice a swede. Soften very thinly sliced onions in a little butter or oil. Layer alternately, adding chopped anchovies and finely chopped dill.

Celeriac and duck confit

Peel and thinly slice a celeriac. Rub a baking dish with duck fat, then layer the celeriac with duck confit (from a can or jar) pulled off the bone, and a little chopped thyme. I like to brown the confit a little in a non-stick frying pan first, then layer it with the sliced celeriac. Bake as opposite. Celeriac can also be used in the bacon version opposite.

Bacon Boulangère

potatoes, smoked bacon, vegetable stock

Scrub **350g large floury potatoes** then slice them thinly, about the same thickness as a pound coin. Remove the rind from **10 rashers of smoked streaky bacon** and cut them into three lengthways.

In an ovenproof dish, layer the potatoes and bacon, seasoning with salt and pepper as you go. Pour in **500ml vegetable stock**, cover the dish with foil and bake for an hour at 200°C/Gas 6. Remove the foil and continue to cook for 15 minutes till brown.

Serve with a crisp salad of iceberg-style lettuce and peppery watercress.

For 4. Frugal, plain and simple. Peaceful starch and soothing stock with a back note of smoke.

Marrow Gratin

marrow, mushrooms, basil, mozzarella,
béchamel sauce, Parmesan

Set the oven at 200°C/Gas 6. Remove and discard the seeds and fibres
from **750g peeled marrow**, then slice into rounds about the thickness
of a pound coin. Warm **a little butter and oil** in a shallow pan. As it
starts to bubble, lower in a few of the marrow slices in a single layer
and let them colour a little underneath. Turn them over and cook the
other side – they should be translucent and tender. Remove them and
drain on kitchen paper. Continue with the rest of the marrow slices.

While the marrow is cooking, thickly slice **300g mushrooms**. When
all the marrow is done, add the mushrooms to the pan, with **a little
more butter** if necessary, season them with salt and pepper, then, as
they are approaching doneness, stir in **15g basil leaves**. Once they
have wilted, remove the pan from the heat.

Cover the base of a large, shallow baking dish with some of the
marrow and mushroom mixture. Tear **a ball of mozzarella** into pieces
and dot them over the mushroom mixture. Spoon **500ml béchamel
sauce** (ready-made is fine) over the surface, then add another layer of
marrow, seasoning as you go. Finally, top with **a generous dusting of
grated Parmesan**. Bake for about 40 minutes, till the sauce is bubbling,
the top gently browned.

For 4–6. A delight for anyone haunted by a marrow in their veg box.

A few thoughts

- Fillet is a lean cut; be generous with the olive oil.
- Use coarse, dry breadcrumbs, ideally the Japanese panko crumbs if you can find them. Scatter any leftover crumbs in the dish and serve them on the side.

Pistou

Spread pistou over the lamb instead of the mustard, and swap the cumin and caraway seeds for herbes de Provence (savory, basil, thyme, lavender). Roast as opposite. On the side: green beans.

Wasabi and panko

Spread the browned lamb with wasabi paste (freshly grated from the root if at all possible) then roll it in the breadcrumbs. Roast as opposite.

Pistachio and black olive tapenade

Spread the warm, sealed lamb fillet with black olive tapenade, roll it in crushed pistachios and roast as opposite.

Harissa and sesame

Spread a layer of harissa paste over the browned lamb, roll lightly in sesame seeds, then roast as opposite.

Mustard

Spread a pork fillet with Dijon mustard and wrap in breadcrumbs the same way as the lamb opposite, but double the cooking time, basting halfway through. Eat with apple purée and a fennel and watercress salad.

Roast Lamb, Mustard and Crumbs

lamb fillets, breadcrumbs, cumin seeds, caraway seeds, Dijon mustard

Trim **a couple of lamb fillets, each weighing about 300g**. Mix **50g dried breadcrumbs, a tablespoon of cumin seeds** and **a tablespoon of caraway seeds** together and set aside. Warm **a film of oil** in a shallow, non-stick pan, season the lamb fillets with salt and pepper then brown them briefly in the oil.

Remove the fillets from the pan and spread them with **Dijon mustard**. I do this quite generously but it depends on your taste for the stuff. Then roll them in the seasoned crumbs. Trickle over **a light coating of olive oil**, then bake for about 10 minutes in an oven preheated to 200°C/Gas 6. Remove from the oven and leave to rest for 5–10 minutes. Slice and serve. Depending on the time of year, green beans, spinach, potato dauphinoise or new potatoes would be an appropriate accompaniment.

For 4. Rose meat. Golden crumbs.

For a change

For a warmer (but far from hot) version, add a pinch of dried chilli flakes to the marmalade mix, or a little finely chopped shallot or onion. Score the chicken all over with a knife, then massage and spread the marmalade down into the slashes.

Mustard, mango chutney, Worcestershire sauce, a spiced chicken sandwich

Mix together a tablespoon or so of Dijon mustard, 2 crushed cloves of garlic, a couple of tablespoons of mango chutney and a tablespoon of Worcestershire sauce. Deeply slash a couple of cold cooked chicken legs, smooth the spice paste over them, then cook under an overhead grill till sizzling. Cut the meat from the bone, then stuff into soft, floury, white baps.

A sweet sticky coating

Make a mixture of runny honey, black treacle, grain mustard and tomato ketchup. The result should be sweet, with a back note of heat from the grain mustard. Toss the drumsticks till well coated, then bake as opposite, keeping a close eye on them. If they appear to be browning too quickly, cover them with foil.

Marmalade Chicken

chicken drumsticks, marmalade,
grain mustard

Put **6 large chicken drumsticks** on a foil-lined baking tray or in a
small roasting tin. Mix **6 heaped tablespoons of marmalade** with
3 tablespoons of grain mustard and a grinding of black pepper.
Spoon the seasoned marmalade over the chicken and bake for about
30 minutes in an oven set at 200°C/Gas 6, keeping an eye on them so
they don't burn.

For 2–3. Sweet, spicy, succulent.

Garlic, shallots, butter and breadcrumbs

In a food processor or by hand, mix 75g butter, a handful of fresh, coarse breadcrumbs, 2 finely chopped shallots, 2 cloves of garlic and a small handful of chopped parsley. Partially cook a couple of oiled, boned chicken thighs or breasts under an overhead, moderately hot grill. As the meat approaches readiness, spread the breadcrumb paste over it and continue grilling, basting occasionally, till golden.

Pancetta and mustard

Blitz a few rashers of pancetta or bacon in a food processor, then mix with soft, fresh breadcrumbs, melted butter and a little Dijon mustard to bind. Spread over the chicken breasts and cook under a moderately hot grill.

Chicken Breast with Smoked Cheese and Pancetta

chicken breasts, pancetta, spring onions, smoked cheese

Slice deeply into the long edge of **2 plump chicken breasts** to give a large pocket in each one. Chop **100g pancetta** into small dice. Fry till crisp in a shallow pan, add **2 chopped spring onions** and continue cooking till the fat is golden, then tip into a bowl. Mix in **100g cubed smoked cheese**, then season with salt and black pepper.

Stuff the filling into the chicken breasts and seal with a wooden skewer or two. Bake in an oven set at 180°C/Gas 4 for 25–30 minutes, till golden. Remove the skewers and serve.

For 2. Golden chicken. Smoky, molten cheese.

Sea bass, waxy potatoes

Place a layer of sliced waxy potatoes in a roasting tin. Toss them with
olive oil, shreds of bacon and a little chopped rosemary. Place a cleaned
whole sea bass on top, rub with oil and rosemary and bake as opposite.

A whole baked fish with aubergines

Cut a couple of aubergines into small cubes of about 1cm or so. Toss
them in plenty of olive oil, salt and chopped thyme. Place in a
roasting tin and bake for about 30 minutes at 180°C/Gas 4, tossing
occasionally so they cook evenly. When they are golden and
thoroughly soft, place a cleaned and prepared whole fish (red or grey
mullet, whole sardines) on top, then trickle generously with olive oil,
the juice of half a lemon and plenty of salt and pepper. Bake till the
flesh of the fish is firm. The exact time will depend on the weight and
variety of your fish, but allow about 20–40 minutes. Serve with extra
oil and lemon.

Baked Red Mullet with Fennel and Leeks

red mullet, fennel, leeks, parsley, lemon

Set the oven at 180°C/Gas 4. Halve and trim **150g young fennel**. If you are using a plump, older bulb, then shred it finely. Trim **150g young leeks**, leaving them whole if they are thin and small; if not, halve them lengthways. Toss the vegetables with **4 tablespoons of olive oil**. Throw in **a little chopped parsley** and **the juice of a lemon**. Tip the mixture into a roasting tin. Place **2 red mullet**, prepared and trimmed, on top of the vegetables. Brush them with oil from the tin, then bake for 20 minutes or so.

For 2. Bright leeks, sweet fish.

Tomatoes with an Anchovy Crumb Crust

tomatoes, anchovies, white bread, basil,
coriander, parsley, spring onions

Set the oven at 180°C/Gas 4. Put **4 tablespoons of olive oil** into a deep
frying pan set over a moderate heat. Slice **6 spring onions** and add
them to the pan. Halve **1kg tomatoes** horizontally and add them to
the pan too. Cover with a lid and cook for 5 minutes or so, till the
tomatoes have softened but are still holding their shape. Add
a chopped tomato to the pan with **a handful of basil and coriander
leaves**, a grinding of black pepper and a very little salt, then turn off
the heat.

Blitz **60g white bread** in a food processor till you have soft, coarse
crumbs, then add **a handful of parsley, 5 anchovies** and a little black
pepper and process again briefly. Transfer the tomatoes and their
cooking juices to an ovenproof dish or tin, scatter the crumb crust
over them and bake for 30 minutes, until the tomatoes are sizzling
and the crust is deep gold.

For 4. Provence!

A thought

Cutting through the chicken requires a good strong knife, but your butcher should be pleased to help if you prefer. The recipe can be used with joints too. Thighs and whole legs probably work best.

Sesame and mirin

Rub chicken drumsticks with butter, salt and pepper and roast them. When brown and almost ready, toss in a mixture of toasted sesame oil and mirin, scatter over a few sesame seeds and continue roasting.

Orange and sherry vinegar

Stir a little sherry vinegar into freshly squeezed orange juice, add a little melted butter, then pour over chicken thighs or a spatchcocked chicken. Tuck the empty orange shells underneath and roast as opposite.

Spatchcock Chicken, Rocket, Couscous

chicken, rocket, couscous, lemon, young garlic,
chicken stock, thyme

Set the oven at 200°C/Gas 6. Place **a medium-sized chicken** on a
chopping board and using a heavy, sharp knife cut through the
backbone and open the chicken out flat. (If you don't fancy doing this
yourself, you can ask the butcher to do it.) Place the chicken, skin-side
up, in a roasting tin. In a small bowl or jar, mix **4 tablespoons of olive
oil** and the **juice of a lemon** (keep the empty shells). Season with salt
and pepper, then add the leaves from **3 or 4 thyme sprigs**. Spoon or
pour the oil mixture over the chicken then add **a further 8 or so
thyme sprigs**. Cut **a head of young garlic** in half and tuck the halves
in around the meat, together with the empty lemon shells.

Roast the chicken for no longer than 45 minutes, by which time the
skin should be golden brown and the juices should run clear when
pierced with a skewer in the thickest part of the flesh.

continued

Remove the roasting tin from the oven and put the chicken on a warm plate, covered with foil, to rest. Tip **500ml chicken stock** into the roasting tin and gently scrape at the roasting sediment left in the tin, letting it dissolve in the stock, then tip in **250g couscous**, spread fairly evenly, cover the tin tightly with foil or a cloth and leave to swell for 10 minutes.

Wash **100g rocket leaves** then mix them into the couscous with a fork, loosening the grains as you fold the leaves in. Add a little salt and pepper as you think fit and perhaps **a little lemon juice** to taste. Cut the chicken into pieces and serve with the rocket couscous.

For 4. Couscous plumped up with the roasting juices and pan crustings. No flavours go to waste.

A late-night sardine supper

Drain a can of cannellini beans, tip them into a pan and add a little butter and olive oil. Warm them over a moderate heat. Open a can of good-quality sardines in olive oil, break them up into large pieces, then fold them into the beans. Add a seasoning of salt, pepper and a little red wine vinegar. Hardly a gourmet feast, but worth a thought when you're hungry and perhaps a little the worse for wear.

The reassurance of a classic

Heat the contents of a can or jar of lentils in a generous amount of olive oil, adding a crushed clove of garlic, some salt and pepper, a few leaves of thyme and maybe a bay leaf or two. Simmer gently, stirring regularly. In a shallow pan, fry half a dozen scallops, or a piece of cod, in foaming butter. Toss in a handful of chopped parsley, add a splash of red wine vinegar and serve with the lentils.

Sea Bass with
Tarragon Flageolets

sea bass, flageolet beans, tarragon,
soft butter, lemon

Mash **150g soft butter** with **a good handful of chopped tarragon leaves**
and **a tablespoon of lemon juice**. Season with salt and pepper and
set aside.

Set the oven at 200°C/Gas 6. Season **a large sea bass or 2 smaller
ones** inside and out. Tuck half the tarragon butter inside the belly
cavity, then lightly seal it closed by threading a wooden skewer or
cocktail stick through it. Place the fish in a roasting tin.

Drain and rinse **two 400g cans of flageolet beans**. Surround the fish
with the flageolets and dot the remaining tarragon butter over the
beans. Wrap a piece of foil loosely over the top, then bake for about
40 minutes, depending on the size of your fish. For the last 15 minutes
of cooking, spoon or brush some of the buttery juices over the fish
and return it to the oven without the foil. Break the fish into 4 pieces
to serve and spoon over the beans and juice.

For 4. Silky fish, soft beans.

Satay Drumsticks

chicken drumsticks, peanut butter, Thai red
curry paste, rice wine vinegar, sesame oil,
tamarind paste, sugar, beansprouts

Set the oven at 200°C/Gas 6. Put **250g crunchy peanut butter** in a
mixing bowl with **2 tablespoons of Thai red curry paste, 2 tablespoons
of rice wine vinegar, 2 tablespoons of sesame oil, 2 tablespoons of
tamarind paste, 3 tablespoons of golden caster sugar** and **400ml
water**. Stir well then pour over **8 large chicken drumsticks** and bake
for about 45 minutes. Remove the drumsticks to a warm plate, toss
150g beansprouts through the sauce left in the tin and serve with the
drumsticks.

For 4. Nutty. Spicy. Delicious fingers to lick.

Squid Stuffed with Judión Beans and Tomato

squid, judión or butter beans, tomatoes,
garlic, rosemary, dry sherry

Peel and finely slice **4 garlic cloves**, then fry in **a thin layer of olive oil**
in a deep frying pan till very lightly coloured. Cut **8 tomatoes** into
roughly 8 pieces each, then add to the garlic, together with the
chopped leaves from **a bushy sprig of rosemary**. Cook for 6 or 7
minutes, till the mixture is soft, fragrant and quite juicy. Season with
salt and black pepper.

Drain **650g judión beans or butter beans** of any bottling or canning
liquor, rinsing them in a colander if you wish, then stir them gently
into the tomato mixture and continue cooking, over a moderate heat,
for 5 minutes. Remove from the heat. Set the oven at 200°C/Gas 6.

Check **4 prepared medium squid**, making sure that they are
thoroughly clean and the transparent quills have been removed from
the body sacs and discarded. Set aside the tentacles. Using a
tablespoon, stuff the squid bodies with as much of the filling as you
can, laying them down slightly apart in a roasting tin or large baking
dish. Spoon any excess filling into the roasting tin.

continued

Pour **300ml dry sherry** around the squid, add **a couple more rosemary sprigs** to the tin and bake for 20–25 minutes, occasionally basting the squid with the sherry. Halfway through cooking, tuck the reserved tentacles around the squid bodies.

Serve the squid and tentacles in shallow bowls or on deep plates, spooning the thin juices around them as you go.

For 4. Heartwarming, glowing red and white, with garlic and tomato.

A few thoughts

- Roast potatoes; very creamy and soft mashed potato; steamed spinach; a handful of rocket dressed with lemon juice.
- Like a pork belly, a breast of lamb has plenty of fat to keep it juicy as it cooks. It needs a generous amount of seasoning.

An alternative spice rub

Make the rub with 3 tablespoons of smoked paprika, 3 tablespoons of cumin seeds and 2 tablespoons of garlic salt. Massage into the scored lamb belly, then trickle with oil and roast as opposite.

Slow-roast
Belly of Lamb

lamb belly, rosemary, yellow mustard seeds,
garlic salt, celery seeds, thyme

Set the oven at 170°C/Gas 3. Lay **a belly of lamb, weighing about 700g,**
out flat, fat-side up, then score with a knife at 1cm intervals. Mix
together **4 tablespoons of chopped rosemary, 3 tablespoons of yellow
mustard seeds, 2 tablespoons of garlic salt, 3 tablespoons of celery
seeds** and **the leaves from 6 small sprigs of thyme**, then rub this mix
into the lamb. Trickle with **olive oil** so the surface is nicely moist, then
roast for 1¼ hours. Briefly rest the meat, then serve in thick slices.

For 4. Savoury, juicy. Frugal and aromatic. 287

Caramelised onions, Parmesan, capers

Peel and thinly slice onions and cook in butter over a low to moderate heat until they are soft and bronze. They should be tender enough to crush between finger and thumb. Stir in grated Parmesan, black pepper and a few capers. Spread over the pastry as opposite, roll and bake.

Smoked mackerel, crème fraîche

Mash smoked mackerel with a fork, fastidiously removing any fine bones, season with pepper and lemon juice, and maybe a caper or two, then mix to a soft but not sloppy paste with a little crème fraîche. Spread over the rectangle of pastry, roll and bake.

Sausage Danish

sausages, puff pastry, fennel seeds, egg

Set the oven at 200°C/Gas 6. Lightly flour a pastry board or work surface, then roll out **375g all butter puff pastry** to a rectangle about 30cm x 20cm.

Remove the skins from **400g breakfast sausages** (slice the skin from one end to the other then peel away from the sausage meat). Spread the sausage meat over the pastry, leaving a small border around the edges. Scatter over **2 tablespoons of fennel seeds**. Brush the edges with **a little beaten egg**.

With the long edge facing you, roll the short sides of the pastry, both left and right, until the rolls meet in the middle. Brush with more beaten egg and press the rolls lightly together. Cut into 8–10 finger-thick slices. Place these flat on a baking sheet and brush lightly with more egg. Bake for 10–15 minutes, till puffed and golden.

Makes 8–10. Viennoiserie for carnivores.

A few thoughts

- Cooking sausages slowly will stop them splitting and will allow a good sticky coat to develop on their skins.
- Once the sausages are browned you can let them finish cooking in the stock.
- After crushing the potatoes with a potato masher, beat them with a wooden spoon to incorporate some air and make them light and fluffy.
- Stir a little grain or smooth Dijon mustard into the gravy at the end.
- Use Madeira or dry Marsala in place of some of the stock.
- Add a couple of sage leaves to the gravy.
- Mushrooms, quartered and fried in a little butter, then stirred into the gravy, would be something to consider, as would a little grated horseradish.

Classic S & M

Lightly brown 6 decent butcher's sausages in a little fat or oil in a heavy pan. Push them to one side and cook 2 peeled and quartered onions, broken into layers, on the other side of the pan. Keep the pieces of onion quite large. Once they are deep gold and caramelised, sprinkle over a generous dusting of flour and allow to brown very lightly. Pour in 250ml rich stock, bring to the boil, season, then simmer for 20 minutes. To make the mash, peel 2 or 3 large potatoes, cut them into large pieces and boil in lightly salted water or steam them till tender enough to mash. Add a thick slice of butter and beat till light and fluffy. Serve with the sausages and onion gravy.

Sausages, Mash and Tomato Gravy

sausages, potatoes, tomatoes, shallots,
stock, double cream, butter

Set the oven at 180°C/Gas 4. Peel **2 banana shallots or small onions**,
quarter them lengthways, then put them in a roasting tin with
6 first-class butcher's sausages. Cut **2 beefsteak tomatoes or large
vine-ripened tomatoes** into quarters and add to the tin with
4 tablespoons of olive oil. Bake for an hour, until nicely browned.

Cut **2 large potatoes** into 6 pieces each, without peeling, then boil
them in deep, salted water till tender. Remove the roasting tin from
the oven, place on the hob and pour in **500ml beef or chicken stock**.
Leave to simmer, stirring regularly.

Drain the potatoes and return them to the pan. Add **50g butter** and
mash with a potato masher. Beat in **4 tablespoons of double cream**
with a wooden spoon and season carefully. Leave on a low heat,
stirring regularly.

Mash up the tomatoes in the gravy with a fork, stirring to dissolve
any roasted pan juices into the sauce. Serve the sausages and gravy
over the creamy mash.

For 2. Bolstering food for a cold night.

Cauliflower-cheese
Baked Potato

baking potatoes, cauliflower, milk, bay leaves,
Parmesan

Prick **4 large floury potatoes** with a fork or skewer to stop them
bursting in the oven, then bake at 200°C/Gas 6 for 50 minutes to an
hour, till the skin is crisp.

Break **a small cauliflower** into large florets, put them into a
saucepan with **750ml milk** and **a couple of bay leaves** and bring to the
boil. Salt lightly, lower the heat and simmer till tender. Remove the
cauliflower and set aside.

Slice the tops off the potatoes and discard. Scoop out the potato
flesh, leaving a sturdy shell of potato skin. Mash the potato flesh with
a fork, then stir it into the milk with **150g grated Parmesan cheese**.
Season generously, stirring well. Return the cauliflower to the sauce,
then pile the mixture into the hollowed-out potato shells, scatter with
more grated Parmesan and return to the oven for 15 minutes or so,
till the filling is thoroughly hot and the top is pale gold.

For 4. Nannying, frugal. Utter bliss.

Chorizo Potatoes

baking potatoes, chorizo, Manchego

Rinse **2 large floury baking potatoes,** salt them all over, pierce them here and there with a fork then bake at 200°C/Gas 6 for about 45 minutes till lightly crisp and cooked right through to the centre.

In a food processor, coarsely blitz **250g cooking chorizo,** then place in a shallow, non-stick pan and fry till sizzling and lightly browned. Slice the top from each potato then scrape out the flesh into the chorizo pan, setting the empty potato shells aside. Continue cooking till the potato colours a little – no seasoning is required.

Chop **100g Manchego cheese** and add to the potato and chorizo, then stuff the mixture back into the empty potato shells, grate a further **25g Manchego** and scatter over the potatoes, then bake for 10–15 minutes.

For 2. A big, bold baked potato for a cold night.

Asparagus, bacon, Parmesan

Boil a bundle of asparagus and drain, then slice each stalk into 3 or 4 pieces. Cut 4 rashers of bacon or pancetta into short strips and fry them in a shallow pan until crisp. Toss the cooked asparagus into the pan, scatter over some grated Parmesan and, just as the cheese starts to melt, divide between 2 plates.

Asparagus, garlic, soy

Mix together 2 tablespoons of dark soy sauce, 2 tablespoons of mirin, a pinch of sugar and a little salt. Fry a bunch of slim asparagus spears in a little oil in a wok till tender. Add a finely sliced clove of garlic. When it has turned golden, add the dressing, bubble briefly and serve.

Asparagus Cannelloni

asparagus, lasagne sheets, béchamel sauce, Parmesan

Set the oven at 180°C/Gas 4. Trim **12 asparagus spears**. Cook **4 fresh lasagne sheets**, measuring roughly 20cm x 10cm, in plenty of boiling water for 5 minutes, then drain and brush with **a little olive oil**.

Place a sheet of lasagne on the work surface, put 3 raw asparagus spears on it, then roll up loosely. Continue with the others, placing them snugly in a baking dish as you go. Pour over **500ml béchamel sauce** (ready-made is fine for this), nicely seasoned.

Bake for 30 minutes, then scatter **50g grated Parmesan cheese** over the top and return to the oven for 10 minutes, till the sauce is bubbling and the Parmesan is lightly coloured.

For 2. Rich. Needs a crisp salad at its side.

Spicy sausage, soft, floury bap

Split chorizo sausages in half lengthways, score their cut sides, then grill till soft and sizzling. Split a bun open for each sausage, spread with mayonnaise and tuck the hot chorizo in together with some crisp salad leaves, such as iceberg lettuce, and watercress.

Sweet potatoes, spicy sausages

Peel and roughly chop a couple of sweet potatoes. Toss with a peeled and roughly chopped onion and 2 tablespoons of olive oil. Roast in an oven set at 200°C/Gas 6 for about 30–35 minutes, then add 4 chorizo sausages, cut into fat coins, and toss well. Return to the oven for 15–20 minutes till all is brown and sizzling. Serve with a bowl of mayonnaise.

Chorizo and Potatoes

chorizo, new potatoes, shallots,
young carrots

Put **200g new potatoes** into boiling water and cook until tender, drain
and slice into thick coins. Set the oven at 180°C/Gas 4.

Split **4 chorizo cooking sausages** in half, score them on their cut
sides, then place them in a roasting tin with **a couple of large banana
shallots**, peeled and halved, their layers separated. Add the cooked
potatoes, and **150g small, young carrots**, thinly sliced. Trickle with
a little oil then bake for 20 minutes, till sizzling.

For 2. Smoky, sweet and piquant.

A creamy chicken lasagne, leftover chicken meat with onions

Soften a couple of onions in melted butter over a moderate heat, add leftover chicken meat (or turkey at Christmas), including all the brown meat from under the carcass and the jelly from the roasting tin. Add fresh thyme leaves or tarragon, double cream or crème fraîche and plenty of seasoning. Layer between sheets of cooked pasta as in the recipe opposite. Finish with grated Parmesan and bake.

Sausage Lasagne

sausages, dried lasagne, cherry tomatoes, large tomatoes, Dijon mustard, double cream, Parmesan

Split open **750g plump, tasty butcher's sausages** and peel off their skins, then put the sausage meat into a bowl. Rub **a little olive oil** on the bottom of a small baking dish. Add **sheets of dried lasagne**, broken into pieces to make them fit roughly into the dish. Roughly chop **350g cherry tomatoes**, and distribute half of them over the lasagne. Cover with half of the sausage meat and then another layer of lasagne. Add the remaining half of the tomatoes then another layer of lasagne and the last of the sausage meat. Slice **2 large tomatoes** and put them on top.

Stir **a tablespoon of Dijon mustard** into **250ml double cream**, season lightly, then pour over the top. Cover with **grated Parmesan**. Bake in an oven set at 200°C/Gas 6 for 45 minutes.

For 4. Rich, luscious and filling. A dish to keep out the cold.

A thought

Change the pasta to suit what you have. With the possible exception of the small soup types, such as orzo, pretty much any variety is suitable for this recipe.

Bucatini with porcini

Soak a handful of dried porcini in warm water for 10 minutes till they have plumped up. Fold the porcini into the cream and pasta, instead of, or as well as, the bacon.

With fresh mushrooms

Slice small chestnut mushrooms and fry them in a little butter and oil till they are golden and slightly sticky. Season with thyme leaves, salt and pepper. Use them in the recipe opposite instead of the pancetta. Add a little parsley too, not too finely chopped; it goes well with the mushrooms.

Spaghetti Bake

spaghetti, streaky bacon, garlic, double cream,
vegetable stock, Parmesan

Cook **500g spaghetti or bucatini** in fiercely boiling water till al dente.
Drain, cool in a colander under running water, then set aside. Cut
12 rashers of smoked streaky bacon or thinly sliced pancetta into
finger-thick pieces. Peel and thinly slice **4 cloves of garlic** and cook
with the bacon in a shallow, non-stick pan till the bacon is crisp.

Put the drained pasta in a mixing bowl with **400ml double cream,
200ml vegetable stock**, the bacon and garlic, then season with salt and
black pepper. Toss everything together then transfer to a baking dish.
Scatter the surface with **a good handful of grated Parmesan** and bake
at 180°C/Gas 4 for about 30 minutes till the surface is lightly golden.

For 4. A savoury tangle.

Pork tenderloin, ponzu dipping sauce

Warm a thin film of oil in a roasting dish, season a pork tenderloin with salt and pepper, then brown it on all sides in the oil. Roast as opposite till the inside is just cooked, then leave to rest. Meanwhile, make a dipping sauce from a mixture of soy sauce, sugar, rice vinegar, finely hashed chillies and a little ponzu sauce. A few beanshoots would be fun here too. Slice the pork thickly and dunk each piece in the sauce.

Pork with Blood Orange

spare rib chops, blood orange, oyster sauce,
dark soy sauce, sugar, chilli sauce, garlic,
oranges, radishes

Set the oven at 180°C/Gas 4. Mix **2 tablespoons of oyster sauce,
a tablespoon of dark soy sauce, a tablespoon of caster sugar** and
a tablespoon of chilli sauce. Stir in **2 crushed cloves of garlic** and the
finely grated zest of a blood orange. Place **300g spare rib chops** in
the marinade and leave for as long as you can before roasting – an
hour if you have it; 5 minutes if not.

Place the pork on a wire rack over a roasting tin, mixing the
marinade with **300ml water** in the bottom of the roasting tin. Put in
the oven and leave to cook for 25–30 minutes, until sticky. Remove
the chops from the oven and let them rest briefly, then remove from
the tin.

Place the roasting tin over a moderate heat, squeeze in the **juice of
a blood orange**, then bring to the boil and let the mixture reduce to a
thick, glossy sauce. Thinly slice **2 oranges** and slice or halve **6 radishes**.
Slice the ribs and serve with the oranges and radishes.

For 2. Sweet, aromatic, sticky pork. Glowing oranges.

A quick gravy

Soak the porcini in 250ml water. Peel and thinly slice 2 medium onions, and soften in butter. Add 2 tablespoons of plain flour, cook for a few minutes then pour in 250ml vegetable stock and the porcini soaking water, then add 150ml Marsala. Simmer for 15–20 minutes over a low heat, then add a couple of pinches of sugar, plus salt and pepper. Serve with the toad.

An aubergine and feta version

Toss a layer of sliced aubergines in a generous amount of olive oil, with chopped thyme, a little dried mint if you have it, and a couple of crushed cloves of garlic. Bake until all is sizzling and soft, then add a block of feta, crumbled into large pieces, and toss gently. Pour in the batter opposite and bake as opposite.

Onion and Mushroom Toad in the Hole

banana shallots, dried porcini, Caerphilly, eggs,
plain flour, milk, grain mustard, groundnut oil,
Parmesan

Peel and halve **6 banana shallots**. Cook them in a shallow pan,
starting with the flat side down, in **a little butter and oil** over a
moderate heat. Leave for about 20 minutes, turning, and letting them
soften till deep golden brown and sticky.

Cut **165g Caerphilly cheese** into cubes. Soak **15g porcini** in cold
water for 10 minutes, then drain. Make a batter, by whisking together
2 eggs, 150ml milk and **150ml water, 125g plain flour, 1 tablespoon of
grain mustard** and a little salt and pepper.

Pour a thin layer of **groundnut oil** into a shallow roasting tin, about
30cm x 24cm, then warm in an oven set at 220°C/Gas 7 till the oil
starts to smoke. Add the sticky onions, the drained porcini and
Caerphilly, then quickly pour on the batter. Add **a handful of grated
Parmesan** and bake for 25 minutes or so, till risen.

For 4. Utterly savoury. Gorgeous.

Potato Wedges with Gorgonzola Sauce

potatoes, Gorgonzola cheese, smoked streaky
bacon, dried chilli flakes, smoked paprika,
double cream

Scrub **1kg medium-sized floury potatoes** but don't peel them.
Cut each in half lengthways, then into thick wedges, 3 or 4 to each
half. Cook in boiling salted water for 15 minutes, until they are
approaching tenderness. Drain and tip into a roasting tin. Set the
oven at 200°C/Gas 6.

Cook **8 smoked streaky bacon rashers** in a shallow pan with **a little
oil** till very crisp. Tip into a food processor, add **a tablespoon of dried
chilli flakes, 4 tablespoons of groundnut oil** and **a tablespoon of
smoked paprika** and blitz till the mixture resembles very fine crumbs.
Tip the crumbs over the potato wedges and toss gently to coat. Bake
for an hour or so, till the wedges are crisp and sizzling.

To make the sauce, warm **250ml double cream** in a small non-stick
saucepan, add **150g cubed or crumbled Gorgonzola cheese** and stir
gently till the cheese has melted. Trickle the warm sauce over the
wedges or serve as a dip.

For 4. Lively, scrunchy, homely and fun.

Root Vegetable Tangle

potatoes, parsnip, carrots, onion, rosemary,
pumpkin seeds

Set the oven at 200°C/Gas 6. Shave **250g potatoes, a large parsnip** and
2 large carrots with a vegetable peeler. Peel and finely slice **an onion**
into rings. Toss the potatoes, parsnips and onion in a large mixing
bowl with **a heaped tablespoon of rosemary leaves, 5 tablespoons of
olive oil** and **2 tablespoons of pumpkin seeds**, then tip on to a baking
sheet. Spread out into a shallow layer. Bake for 20 minutes, till tender
and lightly crisp on the edges.

For 2. A light main course. A side dish for any grilled meat.

Sautéed chicken, porcini and Marsala

Cut a handful of new potatoes in half lengthways. Heat a little olive oil in a large pan, add 4 seasoned chicken pieces and the potatoes and cook until brown and lightly crisp. Add a couple of chopped garlic cloves and colour lightly, then add a handful of soaked dried porcini mushrooms and a little chopped rosemary. Pour in a small glass of dry Marsala and simmer, partially covered with a lid, for about 20 minutes, till the chicken is cooked through. For 2.

Chicken Breasts with Taleggio

chicken breasts, Taleggio cheese,
Parma ham, sage

Set the oven at 180°C/Gas 4. Slice **2 large chicken breasts** in half
horizontally. Arrange the slices snugly on a lightly oiled baking sheet
and season with salt and black pepper. Thickly slice **80g Taleggio
cheese** and place on the chicken pieces. Take **4 thin slices of Parma
ham** and wrap one around each piece of chicken, tucking a couple of
sage leaves into each.

Bake for 10–15 minutes, till the cheese has started to flow and the
chicken is cooked through. Lift carefully from the baking sheet with a
fish slice to serve.

For 4. A riff. And a good one.

A thought

I use the plump, slightly rounded Marcona almonds for this. Rich and sweet, they contribute so much flavour. Whichever type you use, toast them till they are deep gold in colour before adding the liquid.

The basic pot roast

Pot-roasting is a very simple method: a chicken, or some chicken pieces (or even a pheasant or guinea fowl), a few chopped onions or leeks, some woody herbs, a few pieces of potato maybe, and some form of liquid – cider works well, as does white vermouth. Seasoning, some garlic perhaps, and then a tight lid. Into the oven for an hour or two whilst you do something else. A good-natured way of cooking.

Chicken, Sherry, Almond Pot Roast

chicken thighs, new potatoes, salted almonds,
fino sherry, chervil

Set the oven at 200°C/Gas 6. Season **4 large chicken thighs**, then
brown them as evenly as you can in **a little oil** in a casserole set over
a moderate heat. Slice **200g new potatoes** into thick coins and add
them to the pan, letting them colour lightly. Drop in **80g salted
almonds**, allow them to brown until they are a deep gold colour, then
pour in **100ml fino sherry**. Leave to bubble for a few seconds to burn
off the alcohol, then add **100ml water**, cover with a tightly-fitting lid
and roast for 25 minutes. Remove the lid, add **a small handful of
chervil** and serve.

For 2. Deep flavours from a cheap cut. Salty almonds, dry, pale sherry.

Pork Belly, Pistachios and Figs

pork belly, sausage meat, pistachios, figs

You will need **a piece of pork belly, about 2kg in weight**, boned and with its skin scored. Put the pork belly skin-side up on a chopping board and cut it into 6 equal pieces, then slice each piece in half horizontally.

Put **500g good butcher's sausage meat** in a mixing bowl. Roughly chop **100g shelled pistachios** and add them to the sausage meat, then chop **4 figs** and stir them in. Season thoroughly with salt and pepper, then spread the mixture over the bottom halves of the meat and place them snugly in a roasting tin. Place the reserved halves on top, press firmly then roast for 20 minutes at 200°C/Gas 6.

Turn the oven down to 160°C/Gas 3, add **a further 6 figs**, cut in half, and continue cooking for 1 hour till all is soft and succulent.

For 6. Rich, sweet and fruity. A roast for an autumn day.

A thought

It is the interesting texture of these chickpea cakes that makes them such a winner.

Vegetables, chickpeas and a basil paste, a main-course soup for summer

Finely chop an onion, a stick of celery, a small leek and a carrot then soften in a tablespoon or two of olive oil over a moderate heat. They shouldn't be allowed to colour. Add a couple of cloves of crushed garlic, then a chopped courgette. Pour in a litre of vegetable stock, add a couple of bay leaves, then add two drained 400g cans of chickpeas and leave to simmer for about 30 minutes.

Blitz a handful of basil leaves with about 50g grated Parmesan and a couple of tablespoons of olive oil. When the vegetables are tender, serve the soup in shallow bowls and stir in the basil and Parmesan paste at the table.

Chickpeas, tomato, spice and spinach; a thick but light chickpea soup-stew

Roughly chop an onion and let it soften in olive oil over a moderate heat. Add a couple of finely sliced garlic cloves, a finely chopped chilli and 2 teaspoons of garam masala. Continue cooking for a couple of minutes, then introduce a 400g can of chopped tomatoes and a 400g can of chickpeas. Pour in about 300ml vegetable stock and leave to simmer, with a seasoning of salt and pepper, for about 20 minutes till rich and thick.

Wash two large handfuls of spinach, shred into wide ribbons, then stir into the chickpea mixture. Once the spinach has wilted, serve in deep bowls with pieces of crusty bread.

Baked Chickpea Cakes

chickpeas, cannellini or pinto beans, paprika,
garam masala, dried chilli flakes, chives, parsley,
yoghurt, clementine, mint, watercress

Spread **a 400g can of chickpeas**, drained and rinsed, on to a baking
sheet and dust with **a teaspoon of paprika** and **a teaspoon of garam
masala**. Bake at 180°C/Gas 4 till hot, lightly crisp and fragrant – about
10 minutes. Set aside.

Drain and rinse a second **400g can of chickpeas** and **a 400g can of
cannellini or pinto beans**, then using a potato masher, crush both to
a coarse purée. Stir in **a pinch of dried chilli flakes, a tablespoon of
chopped chives** and **a tablespoon of chopped parsley**, a grinding of
salt and pepper, then the toasted chickpeas.

Form the mixture into 8 balls. Lightly oil a baking sheet or line it
with baking parchment, place the balls on top, then brush them with
a little oil. Bake at 200°C/Gas 6 for 20 minutes until crisp outside.

Make a quick sauce by stirring **the zest of a clementine or small
orange** and **a tablespoon of chopped mint** into **200ml yoghurt**. Serve
in a bowl with the chickpea balls and **watercress**.

For 4. Crisp cakes, soft inside. Earthy and homely. 319

Under a crust

Chop, stir, simmer, cool, roll, shape, cut, fit, fiddle, seal, crimp, glaze and bake. I love a homemade pie but it's all too much for a weekday. You could use a fluffy potato crust, but then you still have to peel, chop, boil, butter and mash. It seems too much of an ask after a day's work, but sometimes you just want pie.

Even using a shortcut, the crust should flatter the filling. That is why a cheese and onion pasty made with puff pastry works so perfectly, as does a fruit pie made with a soft, sweet crust or a thin dusting of Parmesan cheese on a creamy pasta bake. It need not be pastry, or even potato. Yes, your pie crust can be a piece of frozen puff pastry laid casually over the entire dish, like a duvet slightly too big for the bed, but it can be grated root vegetables made crisp with butter. It can be thin slices of potato laid over the surface like cobbles, or even a thick layer of thoughtfully seasoned breadcrumbs. All that matters is the contrast between crust and filling.

I use shop-bought puff pastry without apology; it can give me a nicely crusted beef pie within an hour or so. If you need to, the trick is to take it from freezer to fridge first thing, before you go to work. Seasoned breadcrumbs are useful too, and can be made in a food processor or blender at the click of a switch. More organised cooks than myself probably keep some in their freezer. A crust in seconds. They are perfect for a cream-rich sweetcorn pie but also for a pasta and crab bake. A smashed tortilla can work too, though is probably best crowning a filling it feels at home with, such as some sort of bean stew.

The pies in this chapter have crusts made from cheese, breadcrumbs, pastry, root vegetables and tortilla, and the fillings of fish, beef, vegetables, beans and pasta are made from scratch. But it is worth giving a thought to using up leftovers by turning them into a pie. The remains of a vegetable casserole such as a ratatouille can be bolstered with a crumb crust, or a little bit of stew left from the previous night topped with a pastry lid. The crust makes the leftovers go further, lends them a heartiness and gives them a new life.

Yes, a little more time than chucking chicken pieces in a wok but, as I said, sometimes you just want pie.

A few favourites

A hash-brown crust
Coarsely grate a large potato, then peel and thinly slice an onion. Melt a thick slice of butter in a shallow pan, add the potato and onion and let them cook for 10 minutes or so, till they colour slightly. Scatter over a chicken or beef casserole and bake till the crust is golden and crisp.

A Cheddar and crouton crust
Cut thick slices of bread into cubes, discarding the crust, and toss them in a generous quantity of olive oil. Cut thick slices of Cheddar, Gruyère or other firm, nicely sharp cheese and toss with the bread. Pile in one layer on

top of the filling and brown in the oven. You should get crisp croutons floating in little pools of melted cheese. Particularly suited to a vegetable pie.

Parsnip and horseradish crust
Peel and coarsely grate 300g parsnips and add 3 heaped tablespoons of finely grated fresh horseradish. Melt 50g of butter in a shallow pan, toss the parsnip in the butter till it starts to soften, place on top of a beef casserole or stew and bake for 2 hours in an oven set at 160°C/Gas 3.

A cloud of yellow mash
Peel, boil and mash parsnips with butter and a little grated nutmeg and black pepper. Pile on top of your filling in large, cloud-like spoonfuls. Avoid the temptation to smooth the surface.

Slow-cooked Beef Pie with Celeriac Rösti Crust

cubed beef, baby carrots, baby parsnips,
garlic, flour, butter, beef or vegetable
stock, celeriac, fresh horseradish

Season then brown **500g moderately-sized cubes of beef** in **a little oil**
in a pan set over a moderate heat, then add **200g whole, short, young
carrots** and **100g whole young parsnips** and let them brown lightly.
Peel and lightly squash **6 cloves of garlic** and add them to the pan,
then, as they colour, add **2 tablespoons of flour**. Continue cooking till
the flour has coloured, then stir in **500ml beef or vegetable stock**, and
simmer for 10 minutes. Tip the filling into a small pie dish.

Peel and coarsely grate **300g celeriac**, add **3 heaped tablespoons of
finely grated fresh horseradish** then **50g melted butter**. Toss together
gently, place on top of the beef filling and bake for 1¼–1½ hours in
an oven set at 160°C/Gas 3. Steamed kale on the side.

For 4–6. Pie, but with a crisp, grated vegetable crust. Earthy, mild,
wholesome.

A few thoughts

- Without the cream, the dish is fresher tasting but somehow less interesting.
- You could punch up the heat with a teaspoon of bottled green peppercorns.
- A summer dish.
- To the opposite recipe add a couple of handfuls of cooked, shelled mussels.
- Swap the cod for scallops to make a richer, more 'special occasion' pie.
- If cucumber isn't your thing, try button mushrooms that you have first cooked in butter.
- Change the dill to tarragon, chopping the leaves quite finely.
- This pie is wonderful with leeks in it (in place of the cucumber). Slice the leeks, then sweat them in butter, covered with a lid or a piece of greaseproof paper. They will soften and sweeten.

Salmon and Cucumber Pie

salmon, cod, prawns, cucumber, cream,
capers, bread, butter, dill, lemon

Set the oven at 180°C/Gas 4. Blitz **85g white bread** in a food processor
with **a handful of dill** and the **grated zest of a lemon**. Peel, deseed
and chop **a medium cucumber**.

Remove the skin from **300g salmon fillet** and **200g cod fillet**, cut into
large chunks and put in a shallow baking dish with **250g defrosted,
shelled prawns**. Tuck in the cucumber. Sprinkle in **a teaspoon of
capers**. Season, and add **50g butter** in pieces, **150ml double cream** and
then scatter over the crumb topping. Bake in the oven for 25 minutes.
Serve with peas! Spoonfuls of fresh green peas.

For 4. A light, unfussy fish pie for a summer's day.

A few thoughts

- There is some very good, all-butter puff pastry around and it's worth keeping a sheet of it in your freezer. A stew becomes a pie in a heartbeat.
- The filling should be cold before you lay the pastry on top, but I have got away with it before now. Life isn't always perfect.

Chicken breasts, Madeira, the luxury of double cream

Flatten 2 chicken breasts by wrapping them in cling film and hitting them with a rolling pin or cutlet bat, then dust them in a little seasoned flour. Melt a thick slice of butter in a shallow pan, add the chicken, then cook briefly on both sides till golden. Lift out the chicken, add a glass of Madeira to the pan then bubble and stir to dissolve any chicken bits that have been left behind in the pan. When the liquid has reduced to half its original quantity, stir in 4 tablespoons of double cream, season and simmer briefly.

Quick Chicken Pot Pie

chicken, onions, mushrooms, white beer,
all-butter puff pastry, chicken or vegetable
stock, tarragon

Peel and roughly chop **2 onions**. Brown **400g diced chicken** in **a little
oil**, remove, then add the chopped onions and **100g quartered
mushrooms**, letting them brown. Add **3 tablespoons of flour** and
continue cooking for about 5 minutes, then add **330ml white beer**,
300ml chicken or vegetable stock and bring to the boil. Lower the
heat, then add **4 tablespoons of chopped tarragon leaves**, a grinding
of salt and pepper, and simmer for about 10 minutes till thick. Tip
into a baking dish and leave to cool for as long as you can.

Put **a ready-rolled all-butter puff pastry sheet** on a work surface
and, using the dish as a template, cut out a disc to fit the top. Lay the
pastry disc gently on top of the sauce, then cut three slits with the
point of a knife. Decorate with the remaining pastry, cut into leaves
or whatever you fancy. Bake at 180°C/Gas 4 for 30 minutes.

For 4. Sometimes, you just want pie.

More mac and cheese ideas

A classic macaroni cheese recipe is made with about 250g cooked short macaroni and a good 500ml béchamel sauce – I use the ready-made stuff but you could make your own, if you prefer. I add about 75g grated cheese (whatever kind needs using up) to the sauce and top it with a generous scattering of grated Parmesan.

Blue cheese mac

To a classic mac and cheese recipe (made with either a rich béchamel sauce, grated Cheddar and Parmesan or a contemporary version with crème fraîche, fontina and Parmesan), add a soft, ripe blue cheese, such as Gorgonzola.

Leek macaroni cheese

To a traditional cheese-sauce-style recipe, add a stirring of sliced leeks that you have cooked very slowly in a generous amount of butter without allowing them to colour.

Crab Mac and Cheese

brown and white crabmeat, pasta, milk,
double cream, Dijon mustard, grain mustard,
breadcrumbs, Parmesan

Set the oven at 180°C/Gas 4. Boil **250g medium-sized pasta, such as
penne, serpentelli or macaroni**, in deep, well-salted boiling water for
about 9 minutes, till tender. Drain and return to the saucepan, then
add **400ml milk, 250ml double cream, a tablespoon of Dijon mustard**
and **2 tablespoons of grain mustard** and bring to the boil. Lower the
heat, stir in **175g brown crabmeat** and simmer gently, stirring often,
for about 5 minutes.

Stir in **125g white crabmeat**, check the seasoning, then tip into a deep
baking dish. Mix **25g fresh white breadcrumbs** with **25g grated Parmesan
cheese** and bake for 20 minutes, till bubbling round the edges.

For 4. Rich, sweet and unctuous.

You can tweak a sweetcorn pie deliciously

- To the recipe opposite add blanched broccoli, cut into large florets.
- Drop the bacon and use cooked sausage instead, or shredded salami.
- Use canned beans, such as cannellini or haricot, drained of their liquid, in place of half the sweetcorn. The dish is not as sweet this way, but is even more substantial.

Sweetcorn fritters

Make little sweetcorn fritters by draining a can of sweetcorn, tipping it into a bowl, then adding a couple of beaten egg yolks, some salt and black pepper, and enough flour to make a heavy batter. Beat the two egg whites to a stiff froth, then fold into the sweetcorn mixture. Heat butter in a frying pan until sizzling, then drop large spoonfuls of the batter into the pan and cook till golden on the underside. Turn with a palette knife, cook the other side and drain briefly on kitchen paper before eating.

Sweetcorn Crumb-crust Pie

canned sweetcorn, onion, potatoes, smoked
bacon rashers, milk, double cream, parsley,
breadcrumbs, butter

Set the oven at 180°C/Gas 4. Peel and slice **an onion** and let it soften
in **30g butter** over a moderate heat. Cut **350g potatoes** into quite
small cubes and add them to the pan, then cut **8 rashers of smoked
bacon** into pieces the size of a postage stamp, and stir into the onions
and potatoes. When the potatoes are tender, add **200ml milk** and
200ml double cream to the pan with **two 300g cans of sweetcorn** and
continue cooking for 10 minutes.

To make the crust, in a shallow pan melt **50g butter** over a
moderate heat then mix in **a large handful of chopped parsley** and
80g breadcrumbs and leave to colour lightly.

Transfer the sweetcorn mixture to an oven dish, scatter over the
breadcrumb crust and bake for 20 minutes.

For 4. Sweet crunch and cream.

Bacon fat, kale and juniper

Heat some bacon fat or ibérico fat, or if you must, olive oil, in a large pan, then use it to cook a sliced onion. Add a sprig or two of thyme, some lightly crushed juniper berries, a glass of sparkling wine – nothing too extravagant – then add shredded kale and stir briefly before covering with a lid and simmering for 10 minutes. As the kale becomes tender, add salt and pepper. An uplifting dish to accompany a pork-based main course.

Kale bruschetta

Remove the tough stems from the kale. Simmer the leaves in chicken stock for 10–15 minutes till soft and dark, then drain and set both stock and kale aside. Have ready some rounds of hot, toasted sourdough bread. Rub the bread with a cut clove of young garlic, place in a shallow bowl, then spoon over a little of the hot stock. Add the cooked kale, trickle with fruity, verdant green olive oil, and finish with a mean squeeze of lemon and coarse flakes of sea salt.

Gratin of Kale and Almonds

kale, flaked almonds, red onions, cream, béchamel sauce, Parmesan

Set the oven at 200°C/Gas 6. Peel and finely slice **2 red onions** into rounds. Warm **a little groundnut or rapeseed oil** in a shallow pan, then add the onions and fry till soft and, here and there, pale gold. Remove the tender leaves from **400g kale** and chop the coarse stems. Add the chopped stems to the onions and continue cooking till the kale has softened and brightened. Add the kale leaves and stir, cooking for only a couple of minutes, then add **25g flaked almonds**.

Tip the onion and kale mixture into an ovenproof dish, stir **300ml double cream** into **500ml béchamel sauce** (ready-made is fine) with **a good handful of grated Parmesan**, then check the seasoning. Pour over the kale and onion, then scatter with **a little more Parmesan** and **a further 25g almonds**. Bake for 30 minutes, till golden and bubbling.

For 4. A green vegetable. A cheese and cream sauce. The crunch of almonds.

Pinto Beans, Chorizo and Tortilla

chorizo, pinto beans, tortillas, sun-dried
tomatoes in oil, onion, garlic, Cheddar

Slice **450g chorizo cooking sausages** into short lengths. Drain
100g sun-dried tomatoes (keep the oil) and chop them roughly. Fry
the sausage in a shallow pan with 4 tablespoons of the oil from the
sun-dried tomatoes. Peel and slice **an onion**, add to the pan and cook
for 10 minutes till the onion softens, then add **a crushed clove of
garlic**. Drain **a 400g can of pinto beans** and tip them into the pan.
Season, then transfer to a baking dish.

Tear **4 tortillas** into pieces, toss with the sun-dried tomatoes,
scatter over the beans followed by **6 tablespoons of grated Cheddar**.
Bake for 10 minutes at 200°C/Gas 6. Serve with an avocado salad.

For 4. Filling, earthy and fun.

In a wok

In some ways, this is the most exciting kind of quick cooking – at least if the wok is hot enough. The moment the food goes into the pan, there should be a slight sense of danger and fun. Of sizzle and spit, crackle and hiss. There may even, very briefly, be a flame or two. If your heart doesn't beat just a little faster when you start stir-frying, then your wok just ain't hot enough.

Get a thin wok. I use mine mostly for stir-fries, or occasionally for steaming a small fish. The crucial thing is that the steel should be thin. The food needs to sizzle on the hot metal and cook very quickly, which is why we must cut it small. At one time the stir-fry was best left to professionals, but now that modern domestic gas jets are bigger, we can do it successfully at home.

Although this method of cooking fits neatly into the premise of this book, it should be said that it is only the cooking time that is minimal. The preparation will almost certainly take longer than the cooking. A stir-fry of vegetables, for instance, must include the time to peel and shred the ginger and finely chop the garlic and spring onion. The vegetables need to be cut into small pieces or thin slices. Any large chunks will slow down the cooking process, the food will steam rather than fry and your stir-fry will no longer live up to its name.

This remains one of my favourite methods of cooking. I like the speed at which the food browns and the whole sense of fun you get with high-temperature frying. Above all, I love my woks. I have two: a shallow Japanese iron pot with short handles that I use for meals for one (and I suspect is not really a wok at all) and a vast, black Chinese thing from Chinatown that I have had for a decade or more. Both harness incredible heat.

You can cook Thai food in a wok – I have often made a green curry in mine – and they are probably more versatile than they are given credit for. But they are principally for food that needs exceptionally high heat and constant movement round the searing-hot sides of the pan. The clue is in the words stir-fry.

A few favourites

Chicken, mushrooms and beans

Skin a large chicken breast, cut it into thick slices and marinate in a tablespoon each of rice wine and light soy sauce for about 15 minutes. Heat a little groundnut oil in a wok and, just as it starts to smoke lightly, toss in 2 chopped cloves of garlic and a handful of sliced chestnut mushrooms. Fry and stir, briefly and quickly, over a high heat. Stir a dusting of cornflour into the chicken, then add to the pan and continue frying for a couple of minutes. At the last minute, add a handful of raw green beans, cut into short lengths. Stir in a tablespoon of light soy sauce, a little toasted sesame oil and a little pepper. Serve with rice.

Smoked salmon, wasabi

Add beaten eggs to a little fizzing butter, stir with chopsticks, then add folds of smoked salmon, a spoonful of crème fraîche and a dash of wasabi or a few bottled green peppercorns.

Fried prawns, tomato sauce

Into a blender or food processor put a small, roughly chopped onion, a deseeded medium hot chilli, a couple of tomatoes, a tablespoon of light soy sauce and 3 tablespoons of tomato ketchup, then blitz to a thick sauce.

In a wok, heat 2 tablespoons of oil, then fry 2 finely chopped garlic cloves for a few seconds until they are golden then add 2 or 3 large handfuls of raw, shelled prawns and fry for 3 or 4 minutes until they are lightly golden. Stir in the tomato sauce and let it sizzle for a minute or two. Finish with chopped coriander.

Stir-fried Chicken with Cashews and Broccoli

chicken breasts, salted cashew nuts,
thin-stemmed broccoli, five-spice powder, garlic

Remove the skin from **2 large chicken breasts**, then slice the
flesh into thick chunks. Put the chicken into a bowl and toss with
3 teaspoons of five-spice powder. Thinly slice **2 garlic cloves**, add
to the chicken and toss together gently.

Heat **2 tablespoons of groundnut oil** in a wok, then add the spiced
chicken pieces and fry for a couple of minutes, till golden. Add **50g
salted cashews, 200g thin-stemmed broccoli** and **200ml hot water** and
bring to the boil. Cover with a lid and steam for a couple of minutes,
till the greens are tender. You will need a spoon for the juices.

For 2. Crisp greens, crunchy cashews, tender chicken.

You can thicken the juices of a stir-fry by adding cornflour or arrow-
root. I prefer not to, unless I am making a classic dish that requires
it. If you like a thicker sauce, add a couple of teaspoons of Shaoxing
wine and 2 tablespoons of cornflour to the five-spice as you toss
the chicken.

A few thoughts

- The choice of noodles is vast. I tend to use a quick rice noodle for this recipe – either the wok-ready sort or those that require only a short soak in boiling water. Up to you.
- Whether you use cooked or raw prawns, they need cooking for only a couple of minutes. Once a raw prawn has gone from grey to pink, it is cooked. Frozen prawns must be defrosted before use.

The otherworldliness of squid, the homeliness of udon noodles

Use a wider noodle, such as the fat udon. Crush a couple of cloves of garlic with the spring onions in the recipe opposite. Slice a squid into rings and add to the pan. Toss with the noodles, plus chopped coriander, mint, Thai basil – whatever takes your fancy. A sizzling stir-fry of green and white.

Pure, clear chicken noodle soup

Peel a thumb-sized piece of fresh ginger and cut it into matchsticks. Bring a litre of chicken stock to the boil, add the ginger and simmer briskly for 5 minutes. Drop 150g dried noodles into the stock and cook for 3 or 4 minutes, till almost tender. Lift them out with tongs and drop into 2 wide bowls. Add a tablespoon of oyster sauce and 2 tablespoons of light soy sauce to the stock, followed by a couple of small, sweet spring onions, very finely sliced. Simmer for a minute or two longer, then ladle it over the noodles. Shake in a few drops of sesame oil before eating.

Prawns, Noodles and Spring Carrots

prawns, noodles, carrots, spring onions, chilli, ginger, orange juice, dark soy sauce, fish sauce

Scrub **200g spring carrots** and slice them in half lengthways. Steam or boil them for 7–8 minutes, till tender but not soft. Drain and set aside. Soak **150g noodles** according to the instructions on the packet.

Finely slice **3 spring onions**. Halve lengthways and deseed **a medium-sized chilli**, then slice it finely. Peel and grate **a knob of fresh ginger**. Heat **a tablespoon of groundnut oil** in a wok, then add the spring onions, ginger and chilli and fry quickly, tossing and stirring for a few minutes. Add **200g peeled raw prawns**. As soon as the prawns show signs of changing colour, add the carrots. Drop in the noodles, then pour in **125ml orange juice, a tablespoon of dark soy sauce** and **a tablespoon of fish sauce**. Sizzle and serve.

For 2. Sweet and gentle.

Crab, cabbage, yuzu

Finely shred red and white cabbage, then soak in cold water to crisp up. Make a citrus mayonnaise by stirring a few teaspoons of yuzu juice (available from Japanese food stores) into mayonnaise, to taste. Toss the drained and dried cabbage with fresh white and brown crabmeat, the yuzu mayonnaise and a little chopped coriander.

Squid, pea shoot and rocket

Toss hot, grilled squid with whole coriander and mint leaves, rocket leaves and pea shoots. Dress with lime juice, fish sauce, a pinch of sugar and a little chopped red chilli.

Aromatic Pork with Cucumber

pork belly, cucumber, dried shallots, garlic, sesame oil, ginger, sugar, mirin, lime

Blitz **3 tablespoons of dried shallots** with **2 peeled cloves of garlic,
2 tablespoons of sesame oil, a tablespoon of grated fresh ginger**,
and **2 teaspoons of sugar**. Tip into a bowl. Cut **300g boned pork belly**
into thin slices and toss with the blitzed aromatics. Lightly peel
a cucumber and thickly slice into chunky matchsticks. Sprinkle with
2 tablespoons of mirin.

Heat a wok, add **a thin film of groundnut oil**, add the pork and
cook for a few minutes till nicely crisp, then add **a tablespoon of lime
juice**. Toss briefly with the cucumber and eat immediately.

For 2. Aromatic, sizzling pork. The crunch of cucumber.

A few thoughts

- Without the crisp lettuce and a cold beer the dish will be too salty. They are as much part of the recipe as the pork.
- Cubes of pork from the shoulder or leg, lean and firm, are more suited to stir-frying than a fattier cut. Save fat-rich cuts for slow cooking where the fat has time to moisten and enrich the meat.
- Move the ingredients quickly around the pan so the pepper doesn't burn. Use rapeseed or groundnut oil which has a lower flashpoint at high temperatures than olive oil.
- If Szechuan peppercorns prove evasive, you can still make a simple salt 'n' pepper pork without them. It will simply be less aromatic. Include a chopped clove of garlic or 4 chopped spring onions if you wish, or a grated knob of ginger or galangal. A grating of lemon zest at the end will freshen the flavours, and work well with the black pepper.
- Coarsely grated carrot, cut as if for remoulade, would be an idea with the pork, as would a few green beans. Coriander leaves, or fresh mint, are appropriate here too, as is picking the hot meat up with a piece of warm, soft flatbread or romaine lettuce.

Salt and Pepper Pork

cubed pork, Szechuan peppercorns, black
peppercorns, lettuce, mint, coriander

Finely crush **a tablespoon of black peppercorns** and **a tablespoon of
Szechuan peppercorns** using a pestle and mortar or some other
heavy weight, then toss with **500g cubed pork shoulder or leg**. Set
aside for 20 minutes or so. Heat a wok or large frying pan over a high
heat. When the pan is very hot, pour in **2 tablespoons of rapeseed or
groundnut oil** and swirl around the pan. As soon as it starts to
shimmer and slightly smoke, add the pork, together with a
tablespoon of sea salt flakes. Fry at a high temperature, stirring
regularly for 5 minutes or so, till the meat has coloured here and
there. Tip into a warm bowl and serve with **iceberg lettuce** and
maybe **a few mint or coriander leaves**. Ice-cold beer to drink.

For 2. Mouth-popping salty heat. Cool, crisp lettuce.

Pork Belly with Lime and Szechuan Peppercorns

pork belly, Szechuan peppercorns, honey, lime, fresh noodles, chives

Cut **300g boned pork belly** into cubes about 3cm thick. Heat **2 tablespoons of groundnut oil** in a wok, then, when the oil is very hot, add the meat. Brown quickly, then add **2 tablespoons of coarsely ground Szechuan peppercorns**, shortly followed by **2 tablespoons of honey** and **the juice of 2 limes**. Continue cooking, moving the meat around the pan for a couple of minutes, then add **200g thick, soft fresh noodles** and **4 tablespoons of chopped chives**. Let the noodles warm and the chives mellow and soften, then season and eat.

For 2. Sweet, sharp, luscious. The peace of noodles.

Miso, mushroom and beef broth

Dissolve 3 tablespoons of dark miso paste in a litre of boiling water from the kettle. Pour into a saucepan, add 100g fresh enoki mushrooms, 2 red bird's eye chillies, halved, and a tablespoon of dark shoyu sauce. Simmer for a couple of minutes, until the mushrooms are soft, with a slightly jellied texture. Pour into 2 deep bowls and add a small handful of coriander leaves to each. Serve piping hot, with 100g raw fillet, rump or rib-eye beef, sliced paper-thin, dipping the slices into the broth for a few seconds before eating. Serve with soup spoons for the broth.

Light, umami-rich broth, tender beef. A bowl to restore, heal and warm. For 2.

Soba Noodles,
Salmon and Prawns

soba noodles, salmon, prawns, chilli, dark soy
sauce, fish sauce, chives, coriander

Bring a large pan of water to the boil. Salt the water generously, add
200g soba noodles and boil for 6 minutes. (Ignore the packet
instructions, because the noodles will get a bit more cooking later.)
Drain and cool under running water.

Cut **450g salmon** into finger-thick strips. Finely slice **a red chilli** but
leave the seeds in – you want a little heat in this dish. Put a large wok
over a very hot flame, leave for a second or two, pour in **1 tablespoon
of groundnut oil**, swirl it round, then add the salmon and **250g large
peeled raw prawns**. Add the finely sliced chilli. Drop in the partially
cooked noodles, continue to stir and fry. The salmon may break up a
bit but no matter.

Add **a tablespoon of dark soy sauce** and **a tablespoon of fish sauce**,
2 tablespoons of chopped chives and **a handful of torn coriander**,
sizzle briefly, and serve.

For 4. Homely noodles, luxurious seafood.

Sirloin, garlic and courgette

Try fillet or sirloin steak, prepared as in the recipe opposite, but with courgettes cut into matchsticks instead of the mangetout. This is good with a little sliced garlic added with the mushrooms.

Steak and greens

Steak as opposite (or use skirt or chuck steak, if you wish), but use button mushrooms, cut in half to give juicy little nuggets, then add shredded spring greens instead of mangetout. A juicy, messy tangle.

Wasabi Miso Beef

rump steak, wasabi paste, white miso,
fresh Japanese mushrooms, mangetout

Heat **a little groundnut oil** in a wok. Add **a 300g rump steak**, in one
piece, and let it brown nicely on both sides. Remove the steak and
leave to rest. Add **110g small Japanese mushrooms (shimeji or enoki)**
to the pan and move them around as they fry so they pick up all the
juices from the steak. Finely shred **200g mangetout**, add to the pan
and fry for a minute. Add **2 tablespoons of white (shiro) miso**,
2 teaspoons of wasabi paste and **100ml water**. Continue to fry and
stir briefly. Cut the steak into pencil-thick slices and return them to
the pan for a minute or so, keeping the centre of the meat rare.

For 2. The savour of steak, the refreshing crunch of mangetout.

On a plate

I cannot count the times dinner has been a collection of things on a plate. An assembly of ingredients that work together but are not what you could call 'a dish'. It could be as simple as good bread and Cheddar; a salad of ripe, pepper-dusted tomatoes and cool mozzarella; a plate of salami with a jagged piece of airy ciabatta or a store-bought pâté with hot toast. And talking of toast, my dinner has been that many a time, albeit with a few flat mushrooms cooked in garlic butter on top or perhaps a can of beans gussied up with a bit of chilli. (Others would no doubt mention boiled eggs, tomatoes or eggs scrambled into a fluffy cloud.)

The assembly can also come in the form of a salad. Of cucumber and tuna perhaps; beetroot and air-dried ham; or a sharp apple salad with feta cheese. It may be an artfully arranged mixture of fennel and ricotta, or something with a cooked element such as bulgur wheat with figs and maybe a slice or two of Parma ham on the side.

Stuff that goes pretty much straight on to the plate often includes a raw ingredient at its heart – something so perfect you want to eat it in all its glory. Fresh crab, cool and salty; a quivering ball of milky-white mozzarella; peas from the garden tossed with ham.

These are, by their nature, light meals. A lunch, a quick bite after work before you go out, a simple supper. I value them for their immediacy and lack of fuss. They are instant hits that involve almost no cooking. Dinner without turning on the oven.

Tomatoes, sun-dried tomatoes, feta, balsamic vinegar, basil. Gentle flavours for when you are out of sorts

Tip 200g couscous into a bowl, pour over enough boiling water to cover, then leave for 20 minutes or so, till the grain has soaked up the water.

Marinate a single 250g piece of feta in 2 tablespoons of olive oil and 2 tablespoons of balsamic vinegar for 20 minutes. Chop 300g cherry tomatoes and 50g sun-dried tomatoes and mix them together in a bowl. Crumble the feta into large pieces, then fork them through the grains with the tomatoes and 3 heaped tablespoons of chopped basil leaves. For 4.

Basil, pine nuts, garlic, mozzarella, and lemon-scented olives

Heat 250ml tomato juice with a crushed clove of garlic, then pour it over 125g couscous and cover. Leave for 10 minutes, then fluff the grains gently with a fork.

Make a herb oil by blitzing 100ml olive oil with 15g basil leaves in a blender or food processor. Roughly dice or tear a 125g ball of buffalo mozzarella. Chop a spring onion, a couple of plump, ripe tomatoes and a large handful of parsley and mix with 125g lemon-marinated olives, sliced in half. Toast a handful of pine nuts and chop them. Toss together the mozzarella, parsley, spring onion, tomatoes and olives, then fold in the soaked couscous and trickle with the basil oil. For 2–3.

A crisp accompaniment to ham
Carrot and celeriac make good partners in a remoulade, the carrot introducing a little sweetness to the mineral qualities of the celeriac. Peel a celeriac and 2 or 3 carrots, then shred them into matchsticks about 6cm long. Salt lightly, then toss with a little lemon juice to stop the roots browning. Toss with crème fraîche, Dijon mustard and a dash of wasabi paste. Yes, wasabi paste. Wonderful with slices of air-dried or York ham.

Tuna, aubergine, basil and lemon

Cut a large aubergine into large dice and cook slowly in olive oil in a shallow pan. When it is golden and silkily soft, add 2 finely sliced garlic cloves and continue cooking for a couple of minutes, till the garlic starts to colour. Add a handful of chopped basil and chives. Drain a 160g can of tuna, gently break up the tuna and stir it into the aubergine. Squeeze over the juice of a lemon. Boil 300g spaghetti in deep, generously salted water for 9 minutes. Toss the sauce lightly with the drained pasta. For 4.

Tuna and tomato bruschetta

Toast some sourdough bread and, while it is hot, pile on to it a few slices of ripe tomato, a handful of tuna and a spoonful of salsa verde made in the blender (olive oil, lemon juice, rocket, basil, parsley, anchovy, capers, no garlic).

Tuna and Cucumber Salad

tuna, new potatoes, cucumber, Dijon mustard,
dill, olives, white wine vinegar, sugar

Wipe **240g new potatoes** clean, removing any loose flakes of skin,
then boil them in plenty of salted water till just tender. Lightly peel
a medium-sized cucumber, cut it in half lengthways, then scrape out
the seeds and pulp from the centre with a teaspoon, reserving them
for the dressing. Cut the cucumber into finger-thick chunks and place
in a large mixing bowl.

Make the dressing: put **a mere pinch of caster sugar** in a blender or
food processor, add **a tablespoon of white wine vinegar**, **a tablespoon
of Dijon mustard**, a little salt and pepper and the reserved seeds and
pulp from the cucumber. Pour in **a tablespoon of olive oil** and blitz
briefly to a smooth, creamy dressing. Tip the dressing on to the
cucumber, add **2 tablespoons of chopped dill** and stir gently.

Drain the potatoes, then cut each one into about 4 thick coins. Add the
warm potatoes to the cucumber, along with **125g best-quality drained
canned tuna in olive oil**, turning them over carefully in the dressing so
they are evenly coated. Scatter over **a handful of purple niçoise olives**.

For 2. A light main dish. A summer lunch. The usefulness of a can
of tuna.

A few thoughts

• Whole smoked mackerel are often juicier than fillets.
• You could use broad beans instead of edamame.

Surf 'n' turf

Add a little smoked bacon, cut into postage-stamp-sized pieces, to
the spring onion. Smoked meats work well with oily seafood such as
salmon and mackerel.

A rare treat

An Arbroath smokie, that rare and wonderful dry-salted and smoked
whole haddock, makes a splendid substitute for the mackerel.

Smoked Mackerel with Peas and Edamame

smoked mackerel, peas, edamame beans,
ciabatta, spring onion

Cook **200g edamame beans in their pods** in lightly salted boiling
water for 10 minutes. Drain the beans and pop them out of the pods.
Cook **150g frozen peas** in deep boiling water till tender, then drain.
Flake **300g smoked mackerel** into large pieces. Tear **100g ciabatta
bread** into large pieces and fry them in **3 tablespoons of olive oil** in
a shallow, non-stick pan over a moderate heat till pale gold and
crisp. Chop **a spring onion** and add to the pan, then toss in the
edamame beans and peas, followed by the smoked mackerel. Serve
immediately.

For 2–3. A smoky, green feast.

More bright and crunchy salads

- Raw cauliflower florets, sliced thickly, tossed with cooked prawns, dill, mayonnaise and small pieces of lemon flesh. (Use sweet Italian lemons, remove the peel and underlying white pith, then chop the flesh very finely.)
- Pears, sliced and tossed with air-dried ham, then dressed with cider vinegar, grain mustard and lemon juice.
- Green mango, peeled, stoned and sliced, then tossed with coarsely shredded cucumber, spring onion, radish, mint, coriander, lime juice and a dash of sesame oil.
- Shredded roast chicken, chopped peanuts, beansprouts, finely sliced red chilli, mint leaves and shredded carrot, tossed with a dressing made from equal amounts of mirin, lime juice and fish sauce, sweetened with a pinch of sugar.

Apple, Ginger and Endive

apples, ginger, endive, limes, cider
vinegar, feta, sprouted seeds

Squeeze the juice from **2 ripe, slightly yellowing limes**. Finely grate
into it **2 teaspoons of fresh ginger**, then stir in **a tablespoon of cider
vinegar**.

Thinly slice **2 apples**, Russet or Cox perhaps, then put them straight
into the dressing. Tear up **2 endive**. Toss with the apple, **a handful of
sprouted seeds** and the dressing. Serve with a huge wedge of **feta
cheese** or perhaps the more gentle Ticklemore.

For 4 as a side dish. Fresh, ultra crisp, almost astringent. A dish to
awaken the senses.

A thought

You could cook the beetroot if you prefer, but the salad will be sweeter if you do, and will lose some of its vital crunch.

Warm steamed cabbage, cream and mustard. Crisp bacon

Grill streaky bacon till crisp. Lightly steam some roughly chopped white cabbage leaves and their thick stems. Make a dressing by mixing white wine vinegar, smooth Dijon mustard, olive oil and a little double cream, to taste. Mix the warm, drained cabbage with a generous amount of chopped parsley, then toss in the dressing and crumble the crisp bacon over.

Kohlrabi, blood orange and coppa

Cut a couple of raw kohlrabi into almost paper-thin slices, then leave to marinate in equal amounts of blood orange juice and white wine vinegar for about an hour. Arrange on a serving plate with thin slices of fat-marbled coppa, black olives and a little frisée lettuce, crisped in ice-cold water. Finish with finely grated orange zest.

Raw cabbage, blue cheese, cold roast pork

Finely shred equal quantities of raw white and red cabbage and leave to tighten in iced water for 20 minutes. Make a dressing with groundnut or rapeseed oil, red wine vinegar and crumbled blue cheese – I used one part vinegar to two parts oil. Drain the cabbage, then toss with the blue cheese dressing and thin slices of cold roast pork.

Beetroot and Fennel Slaw with Speck

beetroot, fennel, speck, soured cream,
onion, red wine vinegar

Peel **a large onion**, slice thinly into rings, then put it in a small bowl
with **3 tablespoons of red wine vinegar** and set aside for 20 minutes.
This will remove the harshness from the raw onion.

Peel **300g raw beetroot** – you'll get pink fingers – then slice into the
thinnest possible rounds and place in a mixing bowl. Remove the
fronds from **2 small fennel bulbs** and set aside, then slice the fennel
very finely and add to the beetroot, but do not mix yet.

Put **150ml soured cream** in a small bowl and beat in **4 tablespoons of
olive oil**. Season with salt and black pepper. Drain the onion, discarding
the vinegar, and add it to the beetroot and fennel. Introduce the
dressing, slowly and lightly mixing it into the vegetables (overmixing
will result in a pink salad).

Pile on to a serving dish, add **6 slices of speck** and then the reserved
fennel fronds.

For 2–4. A sweet crunch. The taste of winter.

Crab, Melon and Basil Salad

white crabmeat, melon, red chilli, lime, basil

Slice **a lusciously ripe 1.5kg melon** in half and scrape out and discard the seeds. Cut the melon into manageable sections, then remove the flesh from the thick outer skin in short, thick slices. The shape is up to you, but I tend to go for short, finger-thick pieces. Put the melon into a bowl, then deseed and very finely shred **a red chilli** and place in a small mixing bowl. Pour in **2 tablespoons of olive oil, the juice of a ripe lime** and then shred or tear about **12 basil leaves** and mix them in with a little salt and black pepper. Put the melon pieces into the chilli and basil dressing and mix together gently, trying not to break the fruit.

Check **250g white crabmeat** carefully for any fragments of shell. Place the melon on a serving dish and scatter the crabmeat over the top.

For 2. Shellfish as salty, fresh and bracing as a wave. Sweet, juicy melon.

Cucumber, Fennel
and Ricotta Salad

cucumber, fennel, ricotta, avocado, lemon,
balsamic vinegar, dill, sprouted seeds

Make the dressing: put **2 tablespoons of lemon juice** in a bowl, stir in
a little salt and black pepper, then whisk in **2 tablespoons of olive oil
and 2 tablespoons of sunflower oil**. Add **a few drops of balsamic
vinegar**. Finely chop **3 or 4 sprigs of dill** and add to the dressing, then
taste and check the balance. It should be fresh but not sharp. Add
more balsamic vinegar as necessary.

Peel **half a cucumber**, remove the seeds with a teaspoon, then cut it
into thick slices. Halve and finely slice **a small bulb of fennel**. Peel
and thickly slice **an avocado** and fold all gently into the dressing, then
let everything sit in a cool place for about half an hour (not much
longer though). Add **several tufts of sprouted seeds**, such as radish or
mung beans.

Transfer to a serving dish, place **a large spoonful of ricotta** per
person on top and serve.

For 2. Light, bright, refreshing. A mild, gentle salad.

The classic

There are few salads as sublime as mozzarella, basil and tomato, but I like mine dressed with olive oil that you have blitzed to a thin purée with basil leaves and a dash of red wine vinegar.

With roast tomatoes and thyme

Halve small, ripe tomatoes, trickle over olive oil then season with thyme, rosemary, salt and pepper and cook under an overhead grill. Tuck torn pieces of mozzarella amongst them.

Crumbed and fried

Slice the mozzarella thickly. Dip in seasoned, beaten egg and breadcrumbs, then fry in olive oil till crisp. Lemon wedges. Maybe some thick slices of ripe tomato.

Pancetta-crumbed
Mozzarella Salad

smoked pancetta, mozzarella, tomatoes,
lettuce, basil

Grill or fry **12 thin slices of smoked pancetta** till very crisp, drain
briefly on kitchen paper, then blitz to coarse crumbs in a food
processor. Break **a large ball of buffalo mozzarella** into 4 pieces, then
roll in the pancetta crumbs.

Slice and lightly salt **2 large tomatoes** and place on a plate with
4 small leaves of butterhead lettuce. Blitz **10g basil** with **5 tablespoons
of olive oil** and a little salt and pepper. Place the crumbed mozzarella
on the tomatoes and lettuce, then spoon over the basil dressing.

For 2 as a light lunch. Crisp bacon, soft mozzarella.

Peas and cheese 1

Add raw fresh peas to a salad of watercress and sliced oranges. Crumble feta cheese over and add some fruity olive oil.

Peas and cheese 2

Grate Parmesan cheese into some freshly cooked warm peas and toss with melted butter or olive oil. The cheese will melt very slightly. Great with lamb chops.

Peas and cheese 3

Toss freshly cooked hot peas and skinned broad beans with a firm white cheese such as Ticklemore or Ryefield goat. Throw in some sliced radishes and add an olive oily/lemony dressing.

374

Peas and Ham

peas, ham, pine kernels, dried
chilli flakes, pea shoots

Pod **200g fresh peas**; if you have bought them ready podded, you will
need 100g. Put them in a large bowl. Roughly chop **3 tablespoons of
pine kernels** and put them in a shallow pan with **a teaspoon of dried
chilli flakes** and **50g butter**. Let the pine kernels colour a little.

Tear **150g thick cooked ham** into rough, jagged pieces, add them
to the raw peas and dress with the hot pine kernel butter. Top with
a large handful of pea shoots, if you have them.

For 2. Humble, sweet. A fresh hit of green peas.

A couple of thoughts

- Raw sweetcorn, which I have used here, is less sugary than cooked and has a more satisfying crunch.
- Whole heads of sweetcorn can be peeled, basted with maple syrup and butter and roasted. Turn them from time to time as they cook, then serve with a chicory and toasted pecan salad.

Sweetcorn, Bacon and Parsley Salad

corn on the cob, smoked streaky bacon, parsley, roasted salted almonds

Heat **3 tablespoons of olive oil** in a shallow pan. Slice **4 smoked streaky bacon rashers** into long, thin strips and fry in the oil till almost crisp. Add **50g roasted, salted almonds** and continue cooking for a minute or two. Slice the kernels off **a corn cob** and stir them into the bacon. Mix briefly, so the raw corn is coated with the bacon fat, then toss with **a handful of torn parsley leaves** and serve immediately.

For 2. Sweet, salty and crunchy.

A few thoughts

- A frugal way to use up the spare meat from the Sunday roast, this is also a clever way to celebrate the remains of the Christmas turkey or goose. I pull the poultry meat from its bones in large, bite-sized pieces and only at the last minute to keep it moist and juicy.
- Instant couscous doesn't need cooking. Pour an equal volume of boiling water over the grains and leave for 10 minutes or until the water has been absorbed, then fluff it up with a fork.
- Pomegranate molasses, with its sweet-sour, caramel citrus tang, is available from Middle Eastern grocers and the major supermarkets.

Torn ham, parsley, green lentils, the rough crunch of russet apples

Tear rough, bite-sized pieces of ham into the prepared couscous. Stir through golden sultanas, chopped parsley, cooked and drained Puy lentils and slices of crisp, cold, slightly sharp russet apple.

Roast pork, chilled tangerines, cool mint

Tear pieces of cold roast pork left from the Sunday roast into chunky pieces. Stir them through the soaked and fluffed couscous. Add peeled and sliced tangerines, parsley and shredded mint leaves; no dried fruits but perhaps some of the pomegranate seeds and pistachios.

Turkey or Chicken Couscous

leftover cooked turkey or chicken or goose, couscous, pumpkin seeds, dried cranberries, golden sultanas, pistachios, mint, pomegranate, yoghurt, pomegranate molasses

Pour 2 cups of freshly boiled water from the kettle over **a cup of couscous**, cover with a lid, then leave to plump up until the water has been fully absorbed. Shred **600g cooked turkey, chicken or goose** into large, juicy pieces and put it into a mixing bowl with **2 tablespoons of pumpkin seeds, 2 tablespoons of dried cranberries or cherries, 2 tablespoons of golden sultanas** and **2 tablespoons of shelled pistachios**. Season generously with salt, pepper and **chopped mint leaves** then add **the seeds of a whole pomegranate**.

Fluff up the couscous with a fork, then fold in the dry ingredients. Top with **4 heaped tablespoons of yoghurt, a trickle of pomegranate molasses**, more **mint leaves**, and **a few more pomegranate seeds**.

For 2–3. Bejewelled leftovers.

- Use instant couscous. If you have the traditional variety, steam it till tender.
- You can grill the vegetables, if you prefer, or cook them in a shallow pan on the hob. Make sure the vegetables are still warm when you dress them. The vegetables could include courgettes and marinated aubergines (olive oil, garlic). You could also put the cooked vegetables on bruschetta. It would be less of a meal – more of a snack – but still worth a go.
- Swap the couscous for cracked wheat or rice if you prefer.

A cheese and apple couscous

Swell the couscous in hot apple juice. Toss with toasted walnuts, shredded fennel, Cheshire cheese, cubed apples and lots of freshly chopped parsley. A little black pepper, a pinch (no more) of ground cinnamon and a squeeze of lemon to finish. A surprising side dish for leftover roast pork.

Ham and broad beans, mild flavours for a summer's day

Boil a small (500g) ham hock in water for about 40 minutes till tender. Remove from the cooking liquor and set aside. Pour the liquid into a bowl, tip in the couscous, cover and let it swell. Remove the ham from the bone and toss with young broad beans, sliced fennel and chopped parsley. A little olive oil will moisten it nicely.

A herb and rocket couscous

Pour the couscous into a heatproof bowl and add a tablespoon of olive oil. Pour over boiling water or stock, cover and leave to swell. Toss together a mixture of toasted pine kernels, fried finely sliced onions, and an abundance of chopped dill, parsley and mint. The quantity of herbs to couscous should be about equal. Fold the mixture together with handfuls of rocket leaves.

Summer Vegetables with Harissa and Couscous

couscous, cherry tomatoes, red onion,
harissa paste, vegetable stock

Halve **200g mixed cherry tomatoes** and put into a roasting tin. Peel
and slice **a red onion** and add to the tomatoes. Toss the vegetables
gently in **olive oil**, to coat evenly, then bake at 200°C/Gas 6 for
approximately 20 minutes, till the tomatoes have started to burst and
the onions are soft enough to crush between your fingers. Pour
100g couscous into the roasting tin.

Bring **400ml vegetable stock** to the boil, pour over the couscous,
cover tightly with foil, then leave for 15 minutes. Season the couscous
with black pepper, then stir in **a tablespoon of harissa paste**. Serve
the couscous with the roast vegetables.

For 2. Grains to nourish and enliven.

Figs, Bulgur and Blackberries

figs, bulgur wheat, blackberries, walnut oil,
red wine vinegar

Bring **150g bulgur wheat** to the boil in deep, lightly salted water, then
cover the pan and turn off the heat.

Take **150g blackberries** and crush 4 of them in a bowl with a fork.
Stir in **a tablespoon of walnut (or olive) oil** and **2 tablespoons of red
wine vinegar**. Wipe **3 ripe figs**, cut off the stalks, then slice down from
tip to base, not quite cutting through to the bottom. Press the sides
gently to open each fig out like a flower.

Drain any water from the bulgur, then toss the wheat with the
remaining blackberries, the blackberry dressing and the figs.

For 3. Calm grain, bright, fruity dressing. A side dish for ham or
beef, or a light lunch.

With rosemary, on toast

Very hot, crisp sourdough toast, spread generously but not gluttonously with beef dripping, a pinch of very finely chopped rosemary and, should you have some, a smear of roasted garlic.

Slow-baked peppers

Melt beef dripping in a roasting tin, add a few Romano peppers, halved lengthways, and slow roast till they are soft as silk. Pile on to toasted sourdough bread with a handful of rocket.

Onion confit in beef dripping with melted cheese

Warm some dripping in a shallow pan, then add sliced onions and cook over a moderate heat till they are soft, golden and sticky. Stir in some of the dark jelly that lies under the fat, then, as it starts to bubble, add chunks of fontina cheese and let them melt into golden pools. Don't stir, but spoon the strings of soft onions, molten cheese and beef juices on to rough, artisan-type toast.

Beef Dripping
Potato Salad

beef dripping, new potatoes, egg yolks, rocket
or watercress, leftover Sunday roast beef

Halve, but don't peel, **350g new potatoes** and boil until tender. Drain
and leave to cool. Warm **150g beef dripping** in a small pan to melt it.
Put **2 egg yolks** in a mixing bowl, then beat in the warm beef fat a
little at a time, as if you were making mayonnaise. You will need to
do this with a hand-held electric whisk on a high speed. It simply
won't work otherwise. When the mayonnaise is thick, add the cooled
potatoes and a little salt.

Serve on a bed of **rocket or watercress**, then top with the crisp end
of the Sunday roast, **a few slices of rare leftover beef** and the brown
residue and sediment, warmed a little, from the roasting tin.

For 2. Deeply savoury, salty, almost smoky. A sensational end for
the roast.

Feta and cucumber

Clean, piquant, bright. Grated cucumber, black pepper, chopped mint, a few capers and some roughly crumbled feta cheese. Fold gently through thick sheep's or goat's yoghurt and pile on to crispbreads.

Pork pâté and apricots

A rough mound of coarse pork or goose rillettes, a few salted capers and slices of ripe, fresh but still slightly sharp apricot.

Chickpea and anchovies

Tip a drained can of chickpeas into a food processor and add 8 anchovy fillets, a good squeeze or two of lemon juice and a handful of flat-leaf parsley. Blitz, introducing a few tablespoons of olive oil as you go, till you have a coarse, soft paste. Pile on to crispbreads.

Salmon with Roast Garlic and Cream

smoked salmon, garlic, cream, dill, crispbreads

Heat the oven to 200°C/Gas 6. Bake **a head of garlic** for 30–40 minutes, until soft. Squeeze the soft cloves out of their skins into a bowl with your finger and thumb. Gently whisk in **150ml double cream**. Chop **110g dill** (you can do this in a food processor, but give only 3 very short bursts on the pulse button). Stir the dill into the garlic cream. Shred **300g smoked salmon** into long, thin pieces. Toss the salmon in the dressing and pile on to **crispbreads**.

For 2–4. Silky salmon. Crisp bread.

A few thoughts

- Ripe, sweet tomatoes are best for this, to balance the salty qualities of the anchovies.
- You don't need to put salt on the tomatoes, the anchovies are salt enough.
- Use chervil in place of the basil.
- Serve the whole lot as a filling for warm pitta, tipping the cooked tomatoes and crunchy cucumber into toasted pitta pockets.
- Add a crumbling of feta cheese and a few torn basil leaves.

Tomatoes, Cucumber and Anchovy

tomatoes, cucumber, anchovy fillets, tarragon, basil, parsley

Slice **4 large tomatoes** in half and put them on a baking sheet. Trickle over **a little olive oil** and season with black pepper. Take **8 anchovy fillets** and add one to each tomato half. Cook under an overhead grill till hot and lightly toasted.

Peel **a cucumber**, slice down its length, then scrape out the seeds with a teaspoon and discard. Chop the cucumber into thick chunks. Make a dressing for the cucumber by pouring **5 tablespoons of olive oil** into a blender or food processor, adding the leaves from **3 or 4 large sprigs of tarragon**, **5 large basil leaves** and **a few parsley leaves** and blitzing till you have a bright green dressing. Season with salt and pepper and toss with the cucumber.

For 2. Vibrant, refreshing.

A few thoughts

- Sweet-sharp fruits and soft, flat speckled salami make a fine addition to a summer lunch.
- The salad will be at its best if the cherries are cold from the fridge and the tomatoes are not overripe, maybe even slightly sharp. It can also be served as a starter.
- Mozzarella would work well in this salad too.

Cherries, Tomatoes and Salami

cherries, cherry tomatoes, salami, tarragon vinegar

Halve and stone **150g ripe cherries**. Cut **150g cherry tomatoes** in half, then toss them with the cherries. Sprinkle **a little tarragon vinegar** over and set aside for no longer than half an hour. The fruits don't need to be seasoned.

Slice **100g good, peppery salami** very thinly and remove the skin, then tuck amongst the cherries and tomatoes.

For 2. Light, bright, the taste of summer.

A few thoughts

- I use speck for the salad opposite because its flavour holds up well against the broccoli, but you could use any air-dried meat.
- This is also a good way of using up the Sunday roast. Cut the slices as thinly as possible.
- For a less rich version, make a dressing with olive oil, lemon juice and dill instead of the crème fraîche.
- After slicing the potatoes in half, I sometimes toss them in a little sizzling oil or butter to crisp them.

An asparagus and ham salad

Boil or steam asparagus spears, drain them, then add them to the salad opposite instead of the broccoli. I prefer to use chervil or tarragon rather than dill for this, though any of the aniseed herbs will work.

Potatoes, Speck and Sprouting

new potatoes, speck, purple sprouting broccoli,
dill, crème fraîche

Scrub **350g new potatoes**. Bring a deep pan of water to the boil, salt it,
then add the potatoes and cook for 20 minutes or so, till tender.
Drain the potatoes and cut them in half. Finely chop **a few fronds of
dill** and stir into **150ml crème fraîche**, together with a little salt and
pepper. Gently toss the hot potatoes in this dressing.

Trim **100g purple sprouting broccoli**, keeping the most tender
leaves attached, then steam or cook in lightly salted boiling water for
a few minutes, till done to your liking. Drain and toss carefully with
the potatoes, trying not to break the spears up. Serve on plates or in
shallow bowls, tucking **100g thinly cut speck** in amongst the potatoes
and broccoli.

For 2. Deep-green broccoli, smoked ham, dill potatoes. Substantial.

Puddings

Most weekday meals, at least in our house, end with a piece of fruit or a slice of cake. It may be a ripe white peach or a bowl of raspberries. It could be a bulging fig, a pear and a piece of Parmesan, or a plate of cherries with a slice of goat's cheese. Many is the time I have closed a meal with some fine chocolate or some shop-bought ice cream. There might be Turkish delight or possibly a handful or two of almonds I have tossed in sugar and left to caramelise in a shallow pan.

But sometimes there has to be pudding. A cheesecake, a trifle, a crumble or a meringue. Indulgent, wholly unnecessary food of a sweet and sugary kind. That ripe peach could be sliced and dropped into a glass of Muscat; the raspberries could be blitzed and used as a sauce for ice cream or strawberries. The figs could be baked with a glass of Marsala and some brown sugar. But sometimes, there just has to be pudding.

I like the idea of baking a banana in its skin till it blackens, splitting it open and squeezing a ripe passion fruit inside, just as I am all for a baked apple if the oven is on anyway. But there are other shortcuts too:

Blackberries, red wine
Bring a few glasses of red wine to the boil, add a tablespoon of sugar for each one and drop in about 400g blackberries. Cook for a few minutes till the fruit starts to soften, then eat warm.

Baked apples, passion fruit

Score some small apples around their middles and bake at 200°C/Gas 6 for 25 minutes or until they are soft. As they come from the oven, squeeze passion fruit juice and seeds over them. Serve with cream.

Bananas, yoghurt, cream

Peel 4 very ripe, soft bananas and whiz them in a food processor. Scrape into a bowl then fold in 150ml thick, sharp yogurt and an equal amount of very softly whipped double cream. Spoon into glasses and chill.

Raspberries and cream

Make a chilled raspberry fool by putting 300g frozen raspberries into a food processor with 250ml double cream. Blitz briefly. You will have something between fool and ice cream.

Blackberry panettone

Toast slices of panettone till golden. Spread generously with a mixture of mascarpone and softly whipped cream. Pile with blackberries, then dust with icing sugar.

A chocolate sandwich

Grate chocolate generously on to slices of brioche, then sandwich together. Toast on both sides in a shallow pan till the chocolate melts. Dust with icing sugar and eat. (Nutella works too, if you have no chocolate.)

Raspberry ripple sandwich

Crush a mixture of raspberries and blackberries with a fork. Sweeten some softly whipped cream with a little icing sugar and vanilla extract. Toast some brioche or plain white bread till pale gold. Fold the crushed berries lightly through the cream in dark red streaks. Pile on to the crisp, warm toast.

An ice-cream sandwich

Take 2 thin, crumbly oat or shortbread biscuits. Pile with vanilla ice cream, then add a scattering of dark chocolate smashed into thin shards. Put another biscuit on top of each and press together, lightly so as not to break the biscuits. Return briefly to the freezer before eating.

Banana Cheesecake

bananas, ginger biscuits, butter, double cream,
white chocolate, cream cheese, vanilla, lemon

To make the crumb crust, melt **60g butter** in a small saucepan and add
3 tablespoons of double cream. Crush **275g open-textured ginger
biscuits** in a food processor, then stir into the melted butter mixture.
When all the crumbs are moist, set about 3 tablespoons of them aside,
then tip the rest into a 20cm loose-bottomed cake tin and smooth them
gently, but avoid compacting them. You want a loose, crumbly crust.

To make the filling, place a heatproof bowl over a saucepan of
simmering water, making sure the water doesn't touch the base of
the bowl. Break **200g white chocolate** into small pieces and drop
them into the bowl, leaving them, unstirred, to melt. As soon as the
chocolate has melted, turn off the heat, pour in **200ml double cream**
and add **a couple of drops of vanilla extract**. Slowly stir the cream
and chocolate together.

Tip **600g cream cheese** into a bowl and fold the white chocolate
and cream mixture into it. Scoop the filling on top of the crumb
crust, smooth the surface level, then cover with cling film and
refrigerate for at least 3 hours.

continued   399

Banana Cheesecake *continued*

To finish, peel and slice **3 bananas**, toss them in **the juice of a lemon**, then pile them on top of the chilled cheesecake. Scatter over the reserved crumbs (if they have set, then simply break them up a bit first).

For 8. Creamy, vanilla scent, ginger crumbs.

A thought

I know the salad opposite sounds extraordinary but it is the crispest, most refreshing fruit salad imaginable. The strawberries and cucumber work beautifully with the syrup. This is summer in a bowl.

More unusual salads

- Peeled lychees tossed with raspberries.
- Blackberries, raspberries and ripe blackcurrants.
- Watermelon, loganberries and a syrup made from sugar, water and mint.
- Peaches, raspberries, the faintest breath of rose water.
- Mango and passion fruit, perfect partners.

Strawberry and Cucumber Salad

strawberries, cucumbers, honey, mint, elderflower cordial

Put **3 tablespoons of honey, 10 mint leaves** and **5 tablespoons of elderflower cordial** into a blender and blitz to a thick, fragrant syrup. (If you don't have a blender, chop the mint very, very finely, mix it with the honey and cordial, then leave it for an hour. Strain through a fine sieve or muslin to remove the mint.)

Peel **2 medium cucumbers**, slice them in half down their length, then scrape the seeds out with a teaspoon. Dice the flesh finely and put it in a large bowl. Remove the leaves from **450g strawberries**, then slice the fruit in half and toss gently with the cucumber.

Pour the mint and elderflower syrup on to the fruit, stir very gently, then cover and leave in the fridge for about 30 minutes before serving.

For 4–6. The essence of summer, like Pimm's on perfectly mown grass.

Chocolate Oat Crumble

dark chocolate, rolled oats, maple syrup,
apricots, raspberries, elderflower cordial

Set the oven at 180°C/Gas 4. Chop **40g dark chocolate** and mix it with
50g rolled oats and **5 tablespoons of maple syrup**.

Halve and stone **6 apricots** and place them in a shallow ovenproof
pan. Trickle over **4 tablespoons of elderflower cordial**. Let the liquid
bubble over a moderate heat for 3 or 4 minutes, then add **150g
raspberries**.

Scatter the oat mixture over the fruit and bake for 20 minutes, till
the fruit is soft and fragrant and the oats crisp.

For 3. Heady, crisp, luscious.

Irish Coffee Trifle

sponge fingers, Baileys Irish Cream, espresso
coffee, hazelnuts, double cream, mascarpone,
vanilla, dark chocolate

Put **100g sponge fingers** into a serving bowl and pour over **150ml Baileys Irish Cream** and **150ml strong espresso coffee**. Leave to soak. Toast **100g skinned hazelnuts** and chop them in half. Whip **200ml double cream** to soft folds, then fold in **200g mascarpone cheese** and most of the chopped hazelnuts. Spread the hazelnut mixture over the sponge fingers and refrigerate.

Softly whip another **200ml double cream**, flavour it with **a little vanilla extract or a knifepoint of vanilla seeds**, then spread it over the hazelnut and mascarpone cream. Leave, covered, in the fridge for about an hour (20 minutes will do in a trifle emergency).

Scatter the remaining hazelnuts over the cream. Melt **35g dark chocolate** in a small bowl set over a pan of simmering water, then trickle and splatter the chocolate over the surface of the cream. Refrigerate for a few minutes, till the chocolate goes crisp, then bring to the table.

For 6. Deep layers of bliss.

A few thoughts

- If you eat these cookies within an hour of filling, they will remain crisp. But I prefer them the next day, when they become soft and chewy.
- Rather than filling the biscuits with the lemon cream, melt 100g dark chocolate, dip each biscuit halfway into the chocolate, then leave on waxed paper in a cool place to set. Alternatively, trickle melted chocolate randomly over the biscuits (in which case you will need a little less chocolate).
- Crumble the cooled cookies over vanilla ice cream.
- Sandwich the biscuits together with vanilla ice cream instead of lemon curd and mascarpone, returning them briefly to the freezer to set.

Oat and Lemon Cookies

oats, butter, muscovado sugar, egg yolk, flour,
baking powder, mascarpone, lemon curd

Set the oven at 180°C/Gas 4. Dice **120g softened butter** and, using an
electric mixer, beat with **120g muscovado sugar** till light and creamy.
Beat in **an egg yolk**. Mix in together **120g porridge oats or coarse
rolled oats, 90g plain flour, half a teaspoon of baking powder** and a
generous pinch of sea salt.

Divide the mixture into 8–12 pieces, depending on how large you
would like your cookies to be. Roll into balls, then flatten each one
out into roughly the diameter of a digestive biscuit and place them
on a baking sheet lined with baking parchment. They should be quite
thick, so they remain a little chewy after baking.

Bake the cookies for 12–15 minutes, till they are lightly coloured but
not yet crisp. Remove the tray from the oven, leave to cool for a
minute or two, then transfer the cookies to a wire cooling rack. As
they cool, they will crisp up.

To make the filling, put **100g mascarpone cheese** in a mixing bowl
and stir in **100g lemon curd**. Use to sandwich the cookies together.
Makes 8–12.

Strawberry Mascarpone Brioche Toasts

strawberries, mascarpone, brioche, hazelnuts,
sugar, vanilla extract, double cream

Lightly oil a non-stick baking sheet, using a mild or flavourless oil. Put
40g skinned hazelnuts and **80g caster sugar** in a non stick frying pan
with a couple of tablespoons of water and bring to the boil. Let the
mixture bubble until the nuts are pale gold. Do not stir more than
once or twice. Watch them carefully as the colour darkens a little, then
tip them on to the oiled tray. Leave for 10 minutes to cool and crisp.

Slice **20 strawberries** in half. You can remove the leaves if you wish.
Lightly whip **200ml double cream** till thick, then gently fold in **200g
mascarpone cheese** and **a little vanilla extract**. Roughly chop the
sugared hazelnuts and fold half of them into the cream and
mascarpone.

Toast **4 slices of brioche** and spread some of the mascarpone
cream on each slice. Pile the strawberries on top and scatter with the
reserved chopped sugared nuts.

For 4. Soft, sweet toast, berries, cream. Summer.

Mango and Passion
Fruit Mess

mangoes, passion fruits, double cream,
meringue

Whip **300ml double cream** till it stands in soft folds. Crumble **180g shop-bought or homemade meringues** into it, roughly, so you get both large and small pieces, but do not stir.

Peel **2 small, very ripe honey mangoes**, slice the flesh from the stones and chop it into small pieces. Add to the cream and meringues. Halve **6 ripe passion fruits**, then squeeze out the juice through a small sieve into a bowl. Gently, very gently, fold the juice, mango and meringues into the whipped cream. It will need only 2 or 3 stirs at most. You can chill for an hour or so, if you wish.

For 4. Heavenly assembly.

Fig and Ricotta Toasts

figs, ricotta, fruit bread, double cream,
walnuts, honey, rosemary

Tip **4 tablespoons of shelled walnuts** into a shallow pan, add
2 tablespoons of honey and **a bushy sprig of rosemary**, crushing it
in your hand a little as you do. Let the honey bubble for a minute or
2 till it starts to darken slightly, then remove from the heat and set
aside for 10 minutes.

Slice **2 perfectly ripe figs** in half. Stir **4 tablespoons of double cream**
into **4 tablespoons of ricotta**. Lightly toast **2 slices of fruit bread**.

Place the toast on 2 plates, divide the ricotta cream between them,
place figs on each, then spoon over the warm walnuts and honey.

For 2. Figs, ricotta, honey and rosemary. Ancient flavours.
Contemporary twist.

Index

A

beef

Beef dripping potato salad 385
A beef sandwich 23
A burger with attitude 36
The deep savour of beef and noodle broth 45
Gorgonzola, the richest burger 36
Jerk burgers 36
A messy beef hash 22
Miso, mushroom and beef broth 352
Miso soup with beef and kale 71
A mustard and tarragon sauce for steak 80
Philly cheese steak with tagliatelle 115
A red chilli and tomato sauce for steak 81
Ricotta burgers 37
Sirloin, garlic and courgette 354
Slow-cooked beef pie with celeriac rösti crust 325
Steak and greens 354
Steak with miso 137
Steak sandwich 6
Steak sandwich, buttery greens 22
Tomatoes, charred onions and steak 141
Wasabi miso beef 355

beef dripping

Beef dripping potato salad 385
Beef dripping with rosemary, on toast 384
Onion confit in beef dripping with melted cheese on toast 384
Slow-baked peppers on toast 384

beetroots

Beetroot and fennel slaw with speck 367
Beetroot with sausage and rosemary 85
Grilled kippers, beetroot and horseradish mash 169
Roasted beetroot and tomato spelt 7
Spiced root frittata 123

biscuits

Banana cheesecake 399–400
An ice-cream sandwich 397
Oat and lemon cookies 407

black beans

Black bean and onion stew 247
Carrot, black beans and coriander soup 47

black pudding

Black pudding, a cloud of potatoes and apples 90
Black pudding frittata 122
Morcilla burger. Dark blood pudding, white baps 12

blackberries

Blackberries, red wine 395
Blackberry panettone 396
Figs, bulgur and blackberries 383
Raspberry ripple sandwich 397

blood oranges

Kohlrabi, blood orange and coppa 366
Pork with blood orange 305

blue cheese

Blue cheese, figs and a baguette 254
Blue cheese mac 330
Blue cheese, new potatoes 254
Blue cheese rabbit 254
Gorgonzola, pasta, a little olive oil 196
Gorgonzola, the richest burger 36
Onion, quince paste and blue cheese sandwich 24
Raw cabbage, blue cheese, cold roast pork 366
Stewed red cabbage with blue cheese and apple 255

bresaola

Bresaola, Emmental and pickled cucumber sandwich 25

brioche

A chocolate sandwich 396
Raspberry ripple sandwich 397
Strawberry mascarpone brioche toasts 409

Cod with lemon, tarragon and crème
  fraîche 217
Courgette and lemon pasta 196
Couscous, lemons, almonds, squid 171
Pan-fried haddock, parsley sauce, olive oil
  and lemon mash 168
Tuna, aubergine, basil and lemon
  spaghetti 360

lentils
Feta, lentils, olive oil 182
Goat's cheese, lentils, olive oil 182
Lentil bolognaise 183
Lentils with cod or scallops 280
Lentils and golden onions, smoked bacon,
  crème fraîche 182
Lentils, green peas and grilled salmon 182
Smoked haddock with lentils 191
Torn ham, parsley, green lentils, the
  rough crunch of russet apples with
  couscous 378

lettuce
Crisp golden chicken skin, soft green
  leaves, salt flakes 252
A light, fresh, sweet soup for summer 45
Prawns, crisp lettuce and miso 54
Quiet, old-fashioned flavours for leftover
  ham hock 52

limes
Apple, ginger and endive 365
Chicken with dark soy and golden honey,
  chilli fire 148
Chicken thighs, lime and honey 261
Citrus chilli grilled chicken 159
Pork belly with lime and Szechuan
  peppercorns 351

linguine
Brown shrimps, linguine, dill 205

liver
Lamb's liver, onions and Pecorino 107
Liver and bacon ragù 186
The richness of liver, the sweet-sourness of
  apple chutney 106

M

mackerel
Chewy, glossy bagel. Creamy smoked
  fish 192
Green spinach, smoked mackerel, ribbons
  of pasta 192
Mackerel with bulgur and tomato 201
Mackerel wrapped in bacon 180
Smoked mackerel, crème fraîche 288
Smoked mackerel fish cakes 92
Smoked mackerel and green beans 193
Smoked mackerel with peas and
  edamame 363

mangetout
Wasabi miso beef 355

mangoes
Mango and passion fruit mess 411
Pork and mango kebabs 143

maple syrup
Chicken, light soy, smoky chilli flakes, the
  warmth of maple syrup 144
Chocolate oat crumble 403
Pork with apples and maple syrup 261

marmalade
Marmalade chicken 271

marrows
Marrow gratin 267

mascarpone
The bagel 17
Blackberry panettone 396

A note on the type

Typeset in Nexus Mix, a slab serif created by Dutch type designer Martin Majoor in 2004. Nexus is a highly legible, humanistic typeface which takes its name from the Latin word for connection.

The cover is set in Brunel, an English modern designed by Paul Barnes and Christian Schwartz in 2008. Brunel is based on the first moderns issued by the Caslon foundry in 1796. The name is derived from the Anglo-French engineers Sir Marc and Isambard Kingdom Brunel.